Mrs. Edwardes

A vagabond Heroine

Mrs. Edwardes

A vagabond Heroine

ISBN/EAN: 9783337189761

Printed in Europe, USA, Canada, Australia, Japan

Cover: Foto ©ninafisch / pixelio.de

More available books at **www.hansebooks.com**

A VAGABOND HEROINE

By MRS. EDWARDES,

AUTHOR OF

"OUGHT WE TO VISIT HER?" "SUSAN FIELDING,"
"ARCHIE LOVELL," ETC.

"She is too low for a high praise, too brown for a fair praise, and too little for a great praise; only this commendation I can afford her: that were she other than she is, she were unhandsome."—MUCH ADO ABOUT NOTHING.

LONDON:

RICHARD BENTLEY AND SON,
NEW BURLINGTON STREET.
1879.

(All rights reserved.)

A VAGABOND HEROINE.

CHAPTER I.

THE WINE IN THE GRAPE-FLOWER.

SPAIN or Clapham?

A bran-new Clapham villa, all dust, dullness, and decorum, with "Mr. Augustus Jones" upon the bran-new door-plate. A drawing-room, like one's life, oppressively stiff and uninteresting, dining-room to match, husband to match, everything to match. Fine Brussels carpets beneath one's feet; a sun possessing the warmth and cheeriness of a farthing rushlight overhead. Servants to wait upon one and consume one's means; a brougham, perhaps, bearing the Jones coat of arms and liveries; indisputable respectability, indisputable appearance—value, how much of solid good to oneself?—well-maintained. Amusement, pleasure, play, the quick-coursing blood, the jollity, the "go" of existence, nowhere.

So much for Clapham.

And Spain? Spain, just across the Pyrenees there: Spain, from whence the warm wind blows on Belinda's face at this moment: what of that alternative? An uninteresting husband to start with—so much in common have futurity's chances both; but not a stiff, not a dull one. A genial little human creature in the main is Maria José de Saballos, wine merchant and commission agent of Seville; unburthened, 'tis true, by superfluity of intellect, but light of step in waltz and cachuca, and singing tenor love-songs passably; his swarthy fingers too beringed, his swarthy locks too bergamotted, for the very finest taste; his diet overtending, somewhat, towards garlic; and still, if but by virtue of his Spanish picturesqueness, less vulgar far than Mr. Augustus Jones, of Clapham? What would life be by his side?

In the first place, thinks Belinda sagely, life, did one marry the little Sevillian, need not of necessity be passed at his side at all. Maria José would naturally have to look after his agency business, travel to distant countries for wine orders, take his pleasure, as Spanish gentlemen do, in club or café, leaving his wife free—free in a flat in a Seville street; no appearance to keep up, no respectability; a tiled floor instead of Brussels carpet beneath one's feet; not a hope of brougham or liveries this side heaven—but free! The good warmth-giving sun of Spain overhead, a hundred sweet distractions of dance and *tertulia* to count the days by, bull-fights, theatres, and music for one's Sundays: enjoyment, in short, the rule, not the exception of life, and with only Maria José, who, after all, stands comparison with Mr. Augustus Jones right well, for drawback.

Belinda crosses her arms, shakes her head philosophically, yawns a little, then casts herself full-length on the turf, in one of those attitudes of delicious southern laziness which Murillo's beggar children have made familiar to us, and gazing up through the branches of the corktrees at the intense smalt blue of the sky above, begins to meditate.

Sunburnt as a maize-field in June, unshackled bodily, and mentally, by rule as any young Gitana who roams the mountains yonder, through what contradictory whim of fortune came Belinda O'Shea by this high-sounding name of hers? A name reminding one of the musk and millefleurs of boudoirs, of Mr. Pope's verses, china teacups, rouge, pearl powder, artifice! She will be seventeen in a month or two, but possesses few of the theoretic charms assigned by poets and novel writers to that age. Her hands and feet are disproportionally large for her slender limbs; her waist is straight, but formless; her gait and gestures are masculine—no, not that either: to eyes that can read aright the girl is as full of potential womanly grace as is the grape-flower of wine; and still I dare not call her "feminine," as people of the north or of cities understand the word. She can play paume, the national Basque fives or rackets, with any gamin of her stature in St. Jean de Luz; in the excitement of the sport will show hot blood like her comrades; occasionally, indeed —say at some disputed point of a set match—will be tempted into using a very mild gamin's expletive or two; she can row, she can swim, she can whistle. But through her great dark eyes, poor forsaken Belinda, the softest girlish soul still looks out at you with pathetic incongruity, and though her vocabulary be not choice, she possesses heaven's great gift to her sex, a distinctly, excellently feminine voice. Of her possible beauty at some future time we will not now speak. She is in the chrysalis or hobbledehoy stage, when you may any day see a skinny, sallow, ugly duckling of a girl turn into a pretty one, like a transformation in a Christmas piece. Eyes, mouth, feet, hands—all look too big for Belinda at present; and as to her raiment—her tattered frock, her undarned . . . No, I must really enter a little upon the antecedents of my heroine's life before I make known these details, in all the disgraceful nakedness of fact, to the public.

To begin with, the blood of earls and kings (Hibernian kings) runs in her veins. Her mother, the Lady Elizabeth Vansittart, fifth daughter of the Earl of Liskeard, at the romantic age of forty-one fell in love with and married a certain fascinating Irish spendthrift, Major Cornelius O'Shea, whom she met accidentally at a Scarborough ball; endured the neglect, and worse than neglect, of her handsome husband for the space of two years; then, happily for herself, poor soul, died, leaving Cornelius the father of one baby daughter, the Belinda of this little history.

Why Major O'Shea, an easy-tempered, easy-principled soldier of fortune, no longer himself in the freshest bloom of youth—why O'Shea in the first instance should have been at the pains to woo his elderly Lady Elizabeth no one could tell, except that she *was* Lady Elizabeth, and that interest, that *ignis fatuus* of ruined men, might be supposed to lie dormant in the Earl her father's family. Whatever his motives, whatever his matrimonial disappointments, the Major, even his best friends allowed, behaved himself creditably on his wife's death: wore a band that all but covered his hat, swore never again to touch a card or dice-box (nor broke his oath for three weeks), and wrote a letter, full, not only of pious, but of well-worded sentiment, to his father-in-law, from whom, despite many touching allusions to the infant pledge left behind by their sainted Elizabeth, he received, I must say, but a curt and pompous dozen lines in reply. Then, his duties as a widower discharged, Cornelius cast about him to see how he should best perform those of a father. The sum of three thousand pounds, Lady Elizabeth's slender fortune, was settled inalienably on the child. "Me little one is not a pauper entirely," O'Shea would say, with tears in his good-looking Irish eyes. "If Providence in its wisdom should be pleased to sign my recall to-morrow, me angel Belinda would have her mother's fortune to stand between her and starvation." And so, till she had reached the age of seven, "me angel Belinda" was indifferently boarded, at the rate of about forty pounds a year and no holidays, in a Cork convent. Then O'Shea brought his face and lineage once more to the marriage market, on this occasion winning no faded scion of nobility, but the still-blooming widow of a well-to-do London lawyer, and Belinda, for the first time since her birth, had to learn the meaning, bitterer than sweet, poor little mortal, in her case, of the word "home."

No young child it may be safely asserted, was ever unhappy in a community of cloistered nuns. Screen a flower as persistently as you will from the wholesome kisses of sun and light, and if some straggling breath of heaven chance to reach it, not a poor distorted colourless petal but will assert nature in spite of you. Bring women's hearts to a state of moral anæmia by all the appliances priestly science can command, then let little children come near them, and from each pale vestal will blossom forth the instincts of maternity still. If Belinda had never known the exclusive passion of a mother's love, she had known what at seven years of age is probably to the full as welcome—petting and attention without limits. Before she had been a week under the roof of her father and his new wife, the cold iron of neglect, sharper to a child's sensitive nature than any alternation of harshness and affection, had entered her soul.

The second Mrs. O'Shea was a woman whom all the ladies of her acquaintance called "sweet"—you know the kind of human creature she must be? A blonde skin, the least in the world inclined to freckles, blonde hair, blonde eyelashes, eyes of a dove, voice of a dying zephyr. A sweet little woman, a dear little woman, an admirably well-dressed, and what is more, a *well-conducted* little woman, but . . . not fond of children. Nothing could more beautifully befit her character and the occasion than her conduct towards her small step-daughter. "I should never forgive myself if the poor darling grew up without regarding me as a mother," said Mrs. O'Shea, not wholly forgetful, perhaps, that the poor darling could call the Earl of Liskeard grandpapa. "And though the Major is so sadly indifferent on the *most vital* of all subjects, I feel it my duty to bring her at once under Protestant influences." But the Protestant influences established—a grim London nurse in a London back nursery; the discovery made, too, that obdurate aristocratic connections were in no way to be softened through the child's agency—and Belinda, on the score of love, could scarce have fared worse had she been one of the gutter children whom she watched and envied through the prison-bars of her window down in the court below.

Had she been ornamental, the balls of life might have broken differently for her; a rose-and-white, flaxen-curled puppet, sitting beside another rose-and-white, flaxen-chignoned puppet in a brougham, being scarcely less attractive, though on the whole more troublesome, than a good breed of pug. But she was very far indeed from ornamental; a skinny, dark-complexioned child, with over-big eyes looking wistfully from an over-small face, and hair cropped close to the head, *coupé à rasoir*, according to a French fashion often adopted for the younger children in some Irish convents. And so, all fortuitous accidents working together and against her, Belinda was left to starve; her small body nourished on the accustomed roast mutton and rice pudding of the English nursery, and her soul—eager, fervent, hungry little soul that it was—left to starve!

She tried, impelled by the potent necessity of loving that was in her, to love her nurses. But Mrs. O'Shea's was a household in which, notwithstanding the sweetness of the mistress, the women servants shifted as perpetually as the characters in a pantomime. If Belinda loved a Sarah one month, she must perforce love a Mary the next, and then a new Sarah, and then a Hannah. She tried, casting longing eyes at them from her iron-barred prison windows, to love the neighbouring gutter children, happy gutter children, free to make the most of such grimy fractions of earth and sky as fate had yielded them! She tried—no, effort was not needed here : with all the might of her ardent, keen-strung nature, Belinda, throughout those early years of isolation and neglect, loved her father.

Little enough she saw of him. O'Shea had come into a fortune of some thirty or forty thousand pounds by his second marriage, and was spending it like a man—("like a monster," Mrs. O'Shea would declare piteously, when the inevitable day of reckoning had overtaken them. Would she ever have consented to a brougham and men-servants and Sunday dinners—Sunday dinners! with her principles!—if she had known that Major O'Shea was a pauper, not worth the coat he was married in?) Occasionally, twice in three months or so, the fancy would strike Cornelius to lounge, his pipe in his mouth into the child's nursery for a game of romps. On rare occasions, after entertaining some extra fine friends at dinner, perhaps, he would bid the servants bring Miss O'Shea down to dessert, chiefly, it would seem—but Belinda was happily indiscriminative—for the opportunity her presence afforded of airing his connection with the Earl of Liskeard's family ; on a few blissful Sundays throughout the year would take her out, clinging to his hand, happy to the verge of tears, for a walk through the parks.

This was all—the sole approach to parental love that brightened Belinda's lonely child's life ; and as years went on even this scant intercourse between O'Shea and his daughter lessened. Difficulties multiplied round the man: truths of many kinds dawned upon the poor pink-and-white fool whose substance he had wasted. Recriminations, long absences, cruel retrenchments of expenditure, falling off of fair-weather friends—all followed in natural sequence. And then came the crash in earnest ; Belinda's pittance their only certain support for the future. The house in May Fair must be exchanged for one in Bayswater ; the house in Bayswater must give place to lodgings ; the lodgings, from elegance, so-called, must sink to respectability ; respectability to eighteen shillings a week, no extras, and dirt and discomfort unlimited. Belinda, instead of roast mutton and rice pudding, must eat whatever cold scraps chanced to be over from yesterday's meal, and no pudding at all; instead of yawning over French verbs or thrumbing scales on the piano, must run errands, mend clothes, crimp chignons, plait false tresses, and generally make herself the milliner, lady's maid, and drudge of her stepmamma, Rose.

Barring the hair-dressing duties, which, seeing the straits to which they were reduced, goaded her to desperation, I should say the change of fortune affected the girl's spirits but lightly. Children of a certain age rather like catastrophes that cut them adrift from all old landmarks, so long, at least, as the catastrophes wear the gloss of newness. Belinda, by temperament, craved for change, movement, action of any kind, and of these she had far more in Bohemia than Belgravia. She had also more of her father: not a very desirable acquisition, one would say, viewing matters with the eyes of reason; but Belinda, you see, viewed them with the eyes of love—enormous difference!

Cornelius descended the ladder of life with a philosophic, gentlemanly grace that added the last drop of bitterness to Mrs. O'Shea's cup. It was not his first experience of the kind, it must be remembered, and so long as abundant alcoholic resource fail not, 'tis curious with what ease men of his stamp get used to these little social vicissitudes. O'Shea had worn a threadbare coat, had frequented a tavern instead of a club, had drank gin-and-water instead of claret and champagne, before this, and fell back into the old, well-greased groove of insolvency, almost with a sense of relief.

Belinda, who could see no evil in what she loved, thought papa's resignation sublime.

His dress, from shabbiness degenerated to something worse; his nose grew redder, his hours and his gait alike more uncertain. In Belinda's eyes he was still the best and

dearest of fathers, the most incomparably long-suffering of
husbands. "Rose must have her chignons crimped, must
put on her pearl-powder and her silk dresses, just as if we
were rich still," the girl would think, with the blind injustice
of her age, " while papa, poor papa, wears his oldest clothes
and broken boots—yes, and will sing a song at times to his
little girl, and be gay and light-hearted through it all." And
the wisdom of the whole world would not have convinced
her that there could be courage, of a kind, in Rose's crimped
chignon and silk dresses, and cowardice—that worst
cowardice which springs from apathetic despair—in her
father's greasy coat and broken boots and gin-and-water
joviality.

The truth was this: Cornelius knew that his last trick
was made; Rose, that she had the possibility of one still in
her hand—a certain Uncle Robert, crusty, vulgar, rich,
"living retired" in his own villa at Brompton. Very
different would Belinda's story have turned out had this uncle
chanced to be an aunt. The old lady never lived who could
resist the blandishments of Cornelius O'Shea when he willed
to fascinate. Upon the coarse, tough heart, the hardened
unbelieving ears of Uncle Robert, the Irishman's sentiments,
repentance, touching allusions, even, to honour and high
lineage, were alike wasted. Rosie had chosen to throw herself away upon a scoundrel; don't talk to him about birth,
Uncle Robert called a man a gentleman who acted as a
gentleman. Rosie, poor fool, had made her bed and must
lie upon it—for Uncle Robert's language was no less coarse
than his intelligence. Still, let her come to want, let the
scoundrel of a husband decamp, take his worthless presence
to any other country he chose, and keep there, and the door
of Uncle Robert's house would never be closed against his
sister's child. And as the old man had not another near
relation upon the face of the earth, Mrs. Rose knew pretty
well that, O'Shea's disappearance once encompassed, not

only would the door of Uncle Robert's house, but a fair chance of a place in Uncle Robert's will, stand open to her.

A last card, I repeat, was yet to be played by Mrs. O'Shea. She played it well; with that instinctive knowledge of male human nature that you will find in the very shallowest feminine souls. Uncle Robert was a democrat to the backbone; tittle-tattle from the bloated "upper ten" must consequently be tasteful to him, were it but as proof of his own Radical theories; and Rose would prattle in his ear by the hour together, about her ladyship's card debts and his Grace's peccadilloes, and her poor dear O'Shea's intimate connection with the aristocracy. Uncle Robert was as proud of his purse, as any self-made man in England. Nothing swelled him with the righteous sense of solvency like the sight of another's pauperism; still, for *his* niece to have appeared discreditably dressed before the servants, a poor relation, in all the galling indecency of a merino gown or mended gloves, would have exasperated the old man beyond measure. So Rose took excellent care to do her pauperism genteelly. In the most becoming bonnet, the most scrupulously neat silk dress—"the last of all my pretty things, Uncle Robert. Ah, if you knew—can we poor women help being foolish?—if you knew how dreadful it is to one to give up the refinements of life!"—in the most becoming attire, I say, that woman could wear, this simple creature would pay her humble, tearful, conciliatory visits to the Brompton villa, and seldom return without a crisp piece of paper, never entirely empty-handed, to the bosom of her family.

At last, one fine spring morning, came an overture of direct reconciliation, couched in the plainest possible language, from Uncle Robert's own lips. Let Major O'Shea betake himself to America, one of the colonies, anywhere out of England that he chose, solemnly swearing to keep away during the space of two years at least, and Uncle Robert promised not only to receive back his niece to preside

over his house and sit at the head of his table, but to pay
O'Shea the sum of three hundred pounds before his
departure. Enough, surely, to last, if the man had a man's
heart within his breast, until such time as he could gain a
decent independence for himself by work.

Cornelius was absent from home, that is to say from their
dingy lodgings, for the time being when this occurred; had
been absent more than a fortnight, heaven knows on what
mission—I believe he called it the "Doncaster Spring
Meeting," to his wife and daughter. He returned late that
same evening, rather more hiccoughing of speech than usual,
and with just sixpence short for the payment of his cab hire
in his pocket.

Rosie broke the news of her uncle's proffered generosity,
as O'Shea sat drinking his hot gin-and-water after supper,
Belinda mending a very torn stocking with very long stitches
at his side.

"Of course it is impossible," sighed Mrs. O'Shea, with
tears in her meek eyes. "I feel it a duty to mention the
proposal, if only to show the Christian spirit of *my* relations;
but, of course, such a separation would be impossible."

"Impossible, Rosie!" cried O'Shea, his soddened face
brightening. Of so fine and discursive a nature was the
creature's hopefulness, that the bare mention of three hundred
pounds, and of being rid of his domesticities, sufficed to
inspire him with the visions of a millionaire. "Who talks
of impossible? Am I the man d'ye think?—is Cornelius
O'Shea the man—to let his own paltry feelings stand between
his family and prosperity?"

And in less time than it has taken me to write, husband
and wife had made up their minds, heroically, to the sacrifice.
The details were not difficult to agree upon. Cornelius
would seek his fortune in America, "the best country on
earth for a man of resolution and ability;" poor semi-
widowed Rose take refuge at Brompton; Belinda, with the

hundred and twenty pounds a year derived from her mother's fortune, might be considered independent. She should be sent to some moderately expensive boarding-school for the next two years, the term of her father's banishment, and Uncle Robert had considerately said that she might look upon his house as her home during the Midsummer and Christmas holidays.

Belinda independent, Cornelius put upon his legs and offered his freedom, and Rose restored to a pew in church, fine clothes and livery servants—what a touch of the magician's wand was this!

Next day was Sunday. Major O'Shea dyed his whiskers, which he had suffered to grow grey under the cold shade of poverty, brushed up his coat, put on a pair of lavender gloves, and lounged away the afternoon in the park, his hat as rakishly set on his head, his whole air as jaunty, as in the palmiest days of his youth. Madame, after duly attending morning service—for was it not her first duty, said Rose, her eyes swimming, to offer thanksgiving for her own and dear O'Shea's good fortune?—Madame, after attending morning service, betook herself to Brompton, and employed the remainder of the day in talking over events and planning a thousand agreeable domestic comforts for herself with Uncle Robert. Belinda, poor little fool, cried herself white and sick with passionate grief. She did not want respectability or boarding schools, or a home in the holidays. She wanted all she loved on earth, her worthless old father, and was to lose him!

"We really have very different ways of showing our affection," said Mrs. O'Shea, when she returned, well dressed, blooming, full of hope in the future, and found the child crouched down, dinnerless, dirty, her face disfigured and swollen with tears, beside a fireless hearth. "I suppose I shall suffer more than anyone else by your papa's absence, but I do *what is right*. I do not embitter the thorny path of duty still more to his feet"— Rosie had always a fine florid style of metaphor of her own when she tried to talk grand—"by useless tears and lamentations."

From that night on, until the hour of final separation, scarcely more than a week, Belinda kept her feelings better under control. She worked a little purse in secret, upon which you may be sure many a salt tear fell, put in it all her slender hoard of pocket-money, and pushed it into her father's not unwilling hand, on the day of his departure, instinct telling her what kind of gift would to Cornelius be the welcomest token of filial love. When the supreme moment of parting had arrived, she clung to him, shivering, tearless, dumb; while Rosie, whose only feeling was one of cheerful relief, cried almost to the verge of unbecomingness, and uttered every imaginable wifely platitude about the heartrending cruelty of the situation, and the dreadful, dreadful pain that her devotion to duty and to her husband's interests was costing her.

Then came the removal to Brompton : fine rosewood and mahogany ; excellent dinners ; City friends ; Uncle Robert's vulgar, purse-proud talk—all, it would seem, very tasteful to Mrs. O'Shea. And then, less than a twelvemonth after Belinda felt the last kiss of her father's lips, came a New York paper, directed in a strange hand, to Uncle Robert, and containing the bald announcement of Cornelius O'Shea's death. The poor little girl, away at a second-class Brighton boarding-school, was summoned home in haste; the blinds of the Brompton villa were drawn decently close for four days and partially lowered on the fifth, or imaginary funeral day ; Rosie, for second time in her life, veiled her sorrow under the most bewitching weeds. Uncle Robert talked about the mysterious ways of Providence, kept the corners of his mouth well down before the servants, and ere a week was over had made a new will, leaving every shilling he possessed at the unconditional disposal of his dear niece Rose.

O'Shea, in short, in dying had committed by far the best action of his half-century of life, and everybody in the house knew it; everybody but Belinda. Nature has compensations for us all: gives a neglected little daughter to love, to mourn, even a Cornelius O'Shea. Fiercer than ever grew Belinda's rebellion now against Uncle Robert's smart furniture, dinners, butler; all of them bought, she would say, her dark eyes flashing fire through their tears—bought with papa's life. If they had not driven papa away from England he had not died, nor she been desolate. Let them send her away—anywhere on the face of the earth that was *not* Brompton. Yes, she would go to school abroad; to Boulogne, Berlin, as they chose. Only—pathetic stipulation for her age—let her remain away until she was old enough to see after herself in life unaided, and let her have no holidays. And a charmingly opportune chance of gratifying the girl's perverse fancies was not long in presenting itself. Sedulously reading through the educational column of the *Times*, Rose, one morning, with a lightening of the step-maternal bosom came upon the following:

"Rare opportunity for Parents and Guardians.—A Lady of literary attainments, socially unencumbered, and entertaining advanced ideas as to the higher Culture and Destinies of her Sex, offers her society and influence to any young Girl of good birth, for whom improvement by Continental travel may be desired. Terms moderate, and paid invariably in advance. References exchanged."

By the next post Mrs. O'Shea and the lady holding advanced ideas were in communication. They interviewed each other; they exchanged opinions on the Destiny of the Sex; they exchanged references. After some battling the commercial part of the transaction was brought to a close, and Belinda, suddenly submissive to anything that divided her from Rose, Brompton, and Uncle Robert, made her next great step in life.

The name of her new preceptress (of whom more hereafter) was Burke, Miss Lydia Burke; a name not unknown to fame, either in the speech-making or book-making world. And under, or oftener without, this lady's care, Belinda's "culture" has been progressing up to the present time; no material change occurring meanwhile at Brompton save Uncle Robert's death, which took place about three months before the date at which this little history opens. Some smattering of languages the girl, drifting hither and thither over Europe, has picked up; some music and dancing of a vagrant kind; a good deal of premature acquaintance with human nature: life, opened, I fear, at somewhat tattered pages, for her class-book; neglect, not invariably the worst educator, for her master.

A socially unincumbered lady, bent on correcting the mistakes made by her sex during the past six thousand years, and with the Higher Destinies of the future on her soul, could scarcely have time to waste on the training of the one unimportant unit immediately beneath her eyes. In few minds are broadness of vision and capacity for small detail co-existent. The mind of Miss Lydia Burke was of the visionary or far-embracing order: an order quite beyond the wretched details of laundresses and darning-needles. Newton forgot his dinner-hour: could a Miss Lydia Burke be expected to notice the holes...

But this brings me back exactly to the point at which a certain pride in my poor little heroine forced me into retrospection—the holes in Belinda's stockings.

CHAPTER II.

AMBROSIAL CASH.

It is but too obvious that they are a hap-hazard unlawful pair. Belinda darns not, neither does she sew. Her clothes go uncounted to the washerwoman, and return, or do not return, as they list; by natural processes of selection, such as are of tougher fibre than their fellows survive and come together in the end, irrespective of any primitive differences in colour and design. Of these stockings that she now wears, one being grey the other brown, both ragged, it would indeed be hard to conjecture the original stock; nor is their incongruous effect lessened by a well-worn pair of the sandals of the country—*espargottes*, in Basque parlance, linen slippers, roughly embroidered in scarlet, and bound high above the instep by worsted braid. Her frock is of rusty black, texture indescribable; her hat of unbleached coarse straw, so battered out of shape, that one must see it on a human head to recognize it as a hat at all. And she wears her hair in plaits, tight hideous plaits, tied together at the ends, according to the fashion of the Spanish peasants, by a piece of frayed-out, once green ribbon.

Nothing lovely, nothing artistic, even, about her. Yet 'tis a picture that a stranger of discriminative eye could scarce pass unnoticed—this poor little girl, with her tattered frock and illicit stockings and sunburnt high-bred face, audaciously gay one minute as any Paris gamin's, sad the next as that of a woman who already has tasted the fruit of knowledge and found it bitter.

Spain or Clapham? Raising herself lazily from the sward—such mixture of dust and lifeless stalk as here in the south we dignify by the name of sward—Belinda, after several more yawns, draws forth from her ragged pocket a letter, written on sea-green English note-paper, that must certainly have cost the sender double postage, and in a characterless little boarding-school ladies' hand.

"'MY DEAREST BELINDA :'

("Dearest!—for her to call me 'dearest,' when papa himself used to think 'my dear little girl' sufficient! But Rose must be a hypocrite, even in writing.)

"'You will be surprised, and *I hope pleased*, to hear that I am coming all the way to the south of France to see you. I am sure when I look at St. Jean de Luz on the map it quite takes my breath away. I have always had a horror of the Bay of Biscay, and can never sleep in the train, as most people do; and then I am such a coward about strange beds! But of course Spencer will be with me; and as there have been several cases of smallpox close at hand, and I am so frightened about it, Doctor Pickney says the wisest thing I can do is to pack up my boxes and run. I have been vaccinated three times, and, although the doctors say not, I think it always *took a little*. I do hope there is no smallpox about in the south. If you have not been vaccinated already, you might get it done as a precaution before I arrive. I trust dear, you will find me looking pretty well. I am in mourning still, but of course slight, for poor Uncle Robert has been dead three months—indeed, the milliners scold me for wearing it any longer. But I consult feeling, not fashion, in such things; and what can be more becoming than pale lavender silk richly trimmed, or a white sultane polonaise edged with black velvet and *deep* fringe? I wish I knew whether hats or bonnets were best style in foreign watering-places. I have written to the *Queen* to ask, but I am afraid I shall not get the answer before I start. Nothing is seen in London but those large flat crowns, which never suited me, and the Dolly Vardens have got so dreadfully common. Really, as I often say to Spencer, dress is one long trial. Were it not for those I love, I would—but this is a subject on which I dare not trust myself to speak. My dearest Belinda, I shall have news to tell you when we meet of the most deeply interesting nature, affecting the future *of us both*. I am glad you have made acquaintance with Augustus Jones. He is a prime favourite of mine—indeed, he *will* make me correspond with him—young men are so foolish—and as I tell them all, an old woman like me! What you say about his 'vulgarity' is simply ridiculous. How can it matter whether his father sold patent stoves or not? Has a young man money?—not, How was his money made?—is the question the world asks. I only hope he will be still at St. Jean de Luz when I arrive, which may be almost as soon as this letter. Present my compliments to our excellent friend, Miss Burke, and believe me,

"'Your own affectionate mamma,

"'ROSE.

"P.S.—Augustus Jones has a villa at Clapham, *elegantly* furnished, everything in the first style. I have often dined there in his father's time with poor dear Uncle Robert. Augustus will be an excellent *parti*, I can assure you, Belinda, for *any* girl who may be fortunate enough to win him.'"

Belinda crushes the letter together contemptuously, flings it up twice or thrice, ball fashion, into the air, then, thrusts it away, still in its crumpled state, out of sight, and lapses back into castle-building.

"Spain or Clapham?" Just as she has for the third time asked herself this fatal question, an Englishman, in full afternoon Hyde Park dress, emerges from the Hotel d'Isabella, about fifty yards distant from the little Place or square where the girl is sitting, and espying her, approaches.

The new comer is young, florid, not distinctly ill-looking as far as features go, but most distinctly vulgar. The way he wears his hat, his jewelry, his neck-tie—everything about the man, in short, jars on your taste, you know not wherefore. And then he is mosquito-bitten; and mosquito-bites are not wont to improve the expression of the features, or to confer, even on worthier men than Mr. Jones, an air of distinction.

"A villa at Clapham, elegantly furnished—an excellent *parti* for *any* girl who may be lucky enough to win him," thinks Belinda, as the hero of her air-built romance draws near. "What a pity Rose does not appropriate so much good fortune herself! I must see about making the match up as soon as I get them together."

And with this she laughs aloud, not as young ladies who have learnt to do all things prettily laugh, still less as the British school-girl giggles. Shrill, rather, and impish, laughter savouring of malice, not mirth, is the laughter of Belinda O'Shea. Mr. Jones's face, a spot of warm colour at all seasons, has grown to the hue of a well-ripened tomato by the time he reaches her.

"Good afternoon, Miss Belinda. Upon my word you have found out the only bit of shade in the place. Glad to see you find your own thoughts so amusing." Augustus attempts the drawl of the high-bred swell, as he has seen that personage depicted on the stage. Not with very marked success.

Belinda pushes her ragged hat a little further back from

her forehead, stretches out her shabby, sandalled feet in the dust, then, glancing up at Mr. Jones, much as one small boy glances at another with whom he is inclined to quarrel, but whose strength he measures, begins to whistle.

"I thought yesterday you told me you meant to give up that—that slightly unfeminine accomplishment of yours," he remarks, after a minute.

"And I," retorts the girl, "thought you promised never again to make use of that shocking 'Miss Belinda.' If you had pluck enough to say 'Belinda' outright, I could bear it; but as you have not, and as you seem to think it necessary to call me something, do say 'Miss O'Shea.' You have no idea how *caddish* 'Miss Belinda' sounds."

The tomato hue extends itself over poor Mr. Jones's very ears and neck. "Oh! For the future, then, it's to be 'Belinda' between us, is it? Only too happy, on my side, I am sure. But I must ask one thing back." He has taken a place beside her, after carefully selecting a comparatively clean patch of turf on which to deposit his Hyde Park splendour—"I must ask one thing back—that you always call me Augustus."

She looks at him through and through with her fearless child's eyes.

"'Augustus! I hope you have brought me some macaroons, Augustus. Augustus, try not to kick Costa when you think I am not looking.' No, I could not. If I saw you every day till I died, and if I lived to be a hundred years old, I could never call you 'Augustus.' I might do it once"—she corrects herself—"half a dozen times, even, if you bribed me handsomely; but from my heart, never!"

"In other cases you don't appear to feel much shyness about doing so," remarks Mr. Jones, cuttingly. "It seems to me that you call half the English and American fellows in the place by their Christian names."

"Ah! they are only boys," says Belinda, with a smile

brimful of unconscious coquetry. "You would not have me 'mister' my chums—the fellows I play paume with, would you?"

"I would have you not play paume, as you call it, at all," replies the young man, in a tone of deliberate, half-tender patronage. "I like a dash of chic as well as any man" (I am afraid poor Augustus pronounces it chick), "but it must be chic of the right kind, bong tong, and all that sort of thing. Now, what—what should we think in England of a girl who would be seen playing fives as you do, and in such company?"

Belinda shoots a sharp glance at him from under her long lashes. I forgot to mention that the child has long lashes, black as night, too, and overshadowing iron-grey eyes.

"Not play paume, not dance the bolero, not whistle, not take moonlight walks with Costa! What *would* you have me do, I should like to know, Mr. Jones?"

A London beauty of a couple of seasons' standing could not have brought an elder son more neatly and more innocently to the point. Mr. Jones examines the opera dancer who reposes in silver upon the end of his cane, the huge cameo ring that he wears upon his little finger, then he delivers himself of his sentiments thus: "I should like, Miss Belinda—Belinda—I beg your pardon, Miss O'Shea"—for the life of him he cannot get to the familiar Christian name as she sits there in her ragged frock, in her palpable out-crying poverty, and with her little high-bred face held aloft, and her dark eyes mutely dissecting him and his speech to atoms—"I should like to see you the model in all respects of your mamma. My beau idéal—I mean," says Augustus, suddenly recalling recent French lessons, and struggles with French genders, "my belle idéal, of everything most to be desired in an English lady is Mrs. O'Shea."

"Belle idéal! Why can you never let a word alone when by extraordinary accident you have got it right?" cries Belinda, cruelly. "Who ever heard of a belle idéal? Ah!

and so my stepmamma is your beau idéal of everything to be desired in an English lady, and you would advise me to take her as a model in all respects? Thanks. Now I know exactly what courses to avoid and what to imitate. No more paume."

"Paume is the last game I should think an English lady of tong would be seen playing," says Mr. Augustus Jones, oracularly, and giving a contemptuous glance towards the schistera which lies at the girl's side. A schistera, I should explain, is the spoon-shaped basket or hand-shield with which paume is played in the Basque Provinces. "I am quite sure Mrs. O'Shea would think as I do about such a game."

"But then you must remember *I* love it passionately," cries Belinda—"passionately—to distraction! What do I care about being lady-like? If you could play yourself, you would not be such a muff as to talk about 'tong.' Ah! the moment," cries the child, clasping her graceful dark hands—"the moment of moments, when you are twenty all!—the ball with the enemy—you see it spinning through the air—you know that the game is to be made off your own schistera—you strike, you . . . but of course," breaking off, with mild pity of her hearer's ignorance, "of course it's no use talking paume to people who don't understand paume. Well, then comes the bolero. Surely you would allow me one now and then, Mr. Jones, just between the lights, you know, and under shadow of the trees?"

"I don't mind the bolero, or fandango, or any other of the native cancans, provided they are danced by the right people," answers Mr. Jones, with his drawl. "Quite the reverse. When one of these Basque peasant wenches has gone through her barbarous gesticulations, and brings me her tin cup for payment, I put my sous into it with all the pleasure in life."

Belinda's eyes flashed daggers at him. "I cannot imagine your giving a sou to any one on any occasion with pleasure," she exclaims with spiteful emphasis. "And you speak as you do because you know no better! You don't understand the peasants or their dances. You measure everything by your own Clapham tastes, Sir! However, we will not argufy." The reader is asked to pardon this and other linguistic peculiarities on the part of Belinda. "I have my ideas, you yours, and no doubt Rose will back you up in them when she is here. You did not know, by-the-by, that my mamma was coming to St. Jean de Luz, did you, Mr. Jones?"

Mr. Jones hesitates. Talleyrand's advice as to not following one's first impulse for fear it should be a good one, is, although I daresay he never heard of Talleyrand, a first principle with this excellent young man. Prudence, distrust, disbelief in impulse of all kinds, rather than special genius for the development of kitchen grates, raised Mr. Jones, senior, inch by inch, from a shake-down beneath the counter to a Clapham villa and liveries. Prudence, distrust, disbelief in impulse, are qualities born and nurtured in the very life-blood of the son.

"Rose corresponds with you, I know," cries Belinda, scanning his face. "Don't be ashamed of your little weaknesses, Mr. Jones. 'Young men are so foolish,' as Rose says. I can see you know, just as well as I do, that my stepmamma is coming to St. Jean de Luz."

"Well, yes, I know that Mrs. O'Shea is coming here, certainly," says Augustus, deliberation having shown him, perhaps, that to tell the truth, can, for once, cost nothing. "Indeed, I had a few lines from her, written from Paris, by to-day's post. I have her letter in my pocket," where, however, he has the discretion to let it rest. "As far as I can make out, we shall have the pleasure of seeing Mrs. O'Shea and Captain Temple arrive this evening."

Up rushes the crimson in a flood over Belinda's face. "Captain Temple! I don't know what you mean by

Captain Temple!" she exclaims, suspecting what he means only too well, and colouring with hot shame over her own suspicions. "Rose is coming here alone, with her maid, of course."

"Oh, of course!" repeats Augustus, with the slow affected drawl that irritates Belinda to such desperation. "I don't for a moment mean that Mrs. O'Shea, under these or any other circumstances, would act otherwise than with the most lady-like propriety. Still, when one considers everything, Miss Belinda, there is no great wonder in Captain Temple *happening* to travel in the south of France, and in this particular district of the south of France, just at the time when Mrs. O'Shea and her maid *happen* to travel here too!"

His smile, his tone, a sudden scorching remembrance of certain lachrymose allusions in more than one of Rose's recent letters, bring Belinda from suspicion to certainty.

"If I thought—if I could believe such a thing!" she exclaims, then stops short: both sunburnt fists tight clenched, her lips set together like a small fury's.

"If you could believe that two people who loved each other in their youth—I conclude you have heard the romantic story before this?—If you could believe that two people who were in love with each other some dozen or more years ago were fated to marry and be happy at last, what then?" asks Augustus. "Mrs. O'Shea's second marriage would not interfere with your life much, as far as I can see."

"If Rose marries again, I swear never to speak to her or to her husband while I live," cries Belinda tempestuously. "I will not believe such disgraceful news until she tells it me with her own lips, and I have not the very smallest curiosity in the matter. Is he dark or fair?—good heavens, are you dumb, Mr. Jones? What kind of man, I ask you, is this miserable Captain Temple?"

"Roger Temple is fair—yellow, rather; all these Indian fellows are alike—shuts his eyes at you as he speaks—deuced nasty trick for a man to shut his eyes at you as he speaks. I met him once or twice dining at your mamma's before I left town, and we had not two words to say to each other. I don't care for your haw haw Dundreary army men," says Augustus. "Too much of the shop about them for my taste."

"Too much of *what* for your taste?" asks Belinda, with profound disdain. Ah! was not the only human being she ever loved of this same Dundreary army genius as Captain Temple?

"Too much of the shop—their shop. Too much patronage of other fellows whose line doesn't happen to be in ramrods and pipe-clay like their own."

"And I," says the girl, stoutly, "love soldiers; and if ever I marry anybody it shall be a soldier. How different you and I are in everything—difference of the blood, I suppose! We O'Sheas are a fighting family. Two great-uncles of mine fell side by side across the hills there, at Badajoz," she indicates by a nod of her head the distant ridge of Spanish Pyrenees. "And my papa was a soldier; and though it happened he never came in for foreign service, he did a great many brave acts, I can tell you, during the different riots and electioneerings in Ireland. Most likely you have no connection with the army, Mr. Jones?"

"None, excepting a maternal uncle, who was an army tailor," Mr. Jones might answer, if he had a mind to speak the truth. He waives the question adroitly enough, however, by returning to the matter in hand. "Well then, as you are so fond of the fighting profession, Miss O'Shea, you will have an additional reason for loving your new papa."

Belinda snatches up the schistera which lies at her side, and for a moment affairs look threatening. Not much more provocation, evidently, would it need to fire the warlike blood of the O'Sheas that runs in her veins.

"I—I was going to ask you to come down to Harrambour's," says Mr. Jones, springing up hastily to his feet. "Don't be angry with me, Belinda!" He can call her Belinda, at the safe distance that separates them now. "And let us make all our differences up over some macaroons."

Every man, says the cynic, has his price. Belinda's price, as a very short acquaintance has taught Mr. Jones, is macaroons. Sweetstuff, generally, may be said to be Belinda's price in the present scraggy, unfledged stage of her moral life. Angel hair—*cabello de angel*—frozen apricots, chocolate creams, every varied confection, half French, half Spanish, with which the shops of St. Jean de Luz abound, are dear to her. But, above all, she adores macaroons; the speciality of the place, as history shows, even back to the days when the great Napoleon and the English Duke successively lodged here. And then she is so absolutely penniless! The miserable pittance which comes to her quarterly, after Miss Burke has swallowed the lion's share of her small income—the quarterly pittance, I say, which is vouchsafed to her for dress, postage, pocket-money, confectionery, goes so piteously soon, leaves her so absolutely insolvent when it is gone!

A child of seventeen without a sou in the world for macaroons, and an Augustus Jones, his pockets lined with British bank-notes, ready to buy them for her: does it require a very profound knowledge of human nature to foresee how things are likely to end?—unless indeed some other actor, offering something sweeter than macaroons, chance to cross the stage of Belinda's little life-drama.

She hesitates, relents, and a minute later they have quitted the Place, and are making their way down the principal street of the town towards the macaroon shop.

St. Jean de Luz is taking its wonted afternoon siesta at this hour. The balconies are deserted; the very churches, filled morning and evening to overflowing with fans, prayer-books, and flirtations are empty. A bullock-dray or two are to be seen in the market-place, the bullocks in their brown holland blouses, patiently blinking, with bullock philosophy, at existence, the drivers asleep within the wine shops. A team of close-shorn Spanish mules stand, viciously whisking at the flies with their rat tails, in the shade; the muleteer, his face prone to mother earth, reposes beside them. Other living forms are there none, save an occasional half-broiled Murray-guided Briton, and five or six ghostly cur dogs—the cur dogs in St. Jean de Luz *never* sleep. It being low water, the river mouth and harbour are sending forth "liberal smells of all the sun-burnt south." The distant mountain-sides are absolutely painful to the eye in their shadeless ochre yellow. Heat, as of a very rain of fire, quivering, piercing, intolerable, is everywhere.

And Mr. Jones does not bear heat gracefully. By the time they reach the macaroon shop, Mr. Jones is in a state of evaporation made visible, and anathematises the climate, pavement, scenery, people—all in the very ugliest Cockney vernacular, and with the ugliest Cockney ignorance.

"He is horribly, horribly vulgar!" thinks Belinda, as she bites her macaroons, and glances from beneath her eyelashes at the dewy, blistered, mosquito-scarred face of her companion. "If macaroons were only attainable through any other means!"

Which they are not. And the macaroons are super-excellent, fresh made this morning; and after the macaroons come a vanilla ice and a chocolate cream—and more macaroons. And then—of so generous a temper is Augustus this afternoon—then they adjourn from the shop to the refreshing shade of the awning outside, and Belinda is told to call for whatever cooling drink she chooses, while Mr. Jones (who holds the firmest English belief as to alcohol and a thermometer at a hundred and ten in the shade going well together) orders himself—oh, in what execrable French!—a brandy-and-seltzer, and prepares to smoke a cigar at the girl's side.

A bizarre love-making, it may be said, in which the lady's favour is to be won by lollipops. But any one who keeps his eyes open must know that what we call the bizarre differences of life are on the surface—merest accidental diversities of local colouring; human nature being much the same whatever dress she wears, whatever quarter of the globe she inhabits. If Augustus Jones were courting some full-grown London Belinda, his offerings would have to be of bracelets, certainly; bracelets—opera tickets, bouquets, as the case might be, instead of sweetstuff. And who, I should like to know, would consider *that* bizarre?

Mr. Jones smokes his cigar, Belinda sips her iced orangeade, Spanish fashion, through a barquilo, beside him, and so a drowsy hour glides away. Then the sun dips westward behind the toppling old scarlet-roofed, many-storeyed houses that form the seaboard of St. Jean de Luz, and comparative coolness begins to make itself felt in the streets. Little by little shutters open; sleepy faces peep out on balconies; the bullock-drivers come lazily forth from the wine shops; the muleteer rises as far as his elbow, rubs his handsome eyes, swears a little at the mules, crosses himself, and folds a cigarrito. The world is awakening.

"And I must be off," says Belinda, jumping up as the clocks of the town strike five. "We are all in for a match of paume as soon as the sun is off the upper Place."

"We? and who are 'we?'" asks Mr. Jones with a tender smile. The brandy-and-seltzer has softened him; but unfortunately tender smiles lose half their effect when they are associated with mosquito-bites.

"Oh, the usual set. Jack Alston and Tom and me against the two Washingtons and Maurice la Ferté. Which side will you back? You must not judge by what you saw last night; Jack Alston and I can beat the lot when we play our best."

"I should like to bet that you will let Mr. Jack Alston and his friends play their match without you." And now Augustus rises, now the mosquito-bitten face is affectionately, horribly near Belinda's. "I should like to think you care just enough for me, Miss O'Shea, to give all these fellows up for once, if I ask you."

His tone is more earnest than Belinda has ever heard it yet, and she wavers, or appears to waver. The remembrance of macaroons that are past, the hope of macaroons that are to come; vanity gratified by a full-grown man, an Augustus Jones though he be, taking so deep an interest in her affairs;—all these considerations, and, perhaps, something a little deeper than these, sway the girl, and she wavers; casts down her eyelashes, plays irresolutely with the strings of her schistera.

"You will promise me to play no more at that confounded game, either this evening or any other evening?" whispers Augustus, with growing emphasis.

Another moment, and Belinda will certainly have committed herself—heaven knows to what compromising renunciations! But even as the words rise to her lips an unexpected ally, against Mr. Jones, and on the side of paume playing, bolero dancing, and all the other sweet unlawful pleasures of her vagabond life, appears on the scene.

"Costa, why Costa, old boy! where have you been all day? Down, Sir, down. When will you learn that Mr. Jones does not value your attentions?"

Costa is a grand-looking old Spanish hound, not altogether of the purest breed, perhaps, but a noble brute, despite the blot upon his scutcheon, possessing much of his nation's grave dignity of demeanour, and a face brimful of fine dog-intellect and feeling. You may see such a head as Costa's beside the knee of more than one of Velasquez' portraits.

His acquaintance with Belinda came about haphazard—as everything seems to come about in the girl's haphazard life.

Some Madrid hidalgo, to whom the poor brute belonged, happening to be called away to Paris towards the close of last summer's bathing season, the dog, with true Spanish indifference, was left upon the streets of St. Jean de Luz to starve. For a time he kept body and soul—what poor dog-soul was in him—together, as best he might; his lean carcase daily becoming leaner, kicks and blows from housewives who found him unlawfully prowling about their doorsteps more frequent. At last a bone or two came through the skin; the creature's strength was gone—just enough left to drag himself painfully along the gutters, and look up with wistful hungry supplication in the faces of the passers-by.

And so Belinda found him: Belinda, as it chanced, flush of money, her quarter's pittance newly paid, and on her road at that moment to the macaroon shop, with all the lightness of spirit a full purse begets.

"What, Costa, my friend!" She knew the dog and his name well; had admired him often in his palmier days, striding majestically along at the hidalgo his master's heels. "Costa, my old friend, have you come to this? Has that *brute* left you alone here to starve?"

She forgot the macaroons; she took Costa round to the butcher's market, and she gave him to eat; would have had him home and sheltered him, but for Miss Burke's stern opposition. It would better befit Belinda's immortal soul to take thought of the regeneration of humanity than be occupied with the life or death of a miserable cur dog. A knock on the head and a plunge into the Nivelle were the greatest mercy in such a case. Miss Burke, for her part, would not mind hiring some man or boy to perform the deed, and——

"At your peril you get Costa murdered!" cried Belinda, with tragical mutinous eyes. "Deny him shelter, if you like. He must lodge as the beggars lodge, at least till winter comes, and I will feed him. What do I care for humanity? I love the dog! And as for you . . . . hire an assassin, make yourself accomplice in a murder, madam, at your peril!"

Thus doubly saving Costa's life, of such slender value as the poor life was!

And the creature repaid her with that absolute, blind, unstinted gratitude, that is one of the cardinal dog virtues— shall we say an exclusive dog virtue? Without a word of explanation he understood the delicacy of the relations between himself and Miss Burke, yet, for Belinda's sake, never betrayed his knowledge otherwise than by a stealthy, ghastly roll of the eye or grin of the upper lip in that lady's presence. Of a morning he would sit, demure of demeanour as a bishop, outside the gateway of Miss Burke's lodging, waiting for the light step of his little benefactress, but shifting his quarters instantly, and with an air of the most Pharisaic innocence, if Miss Burke chanced to appear instead of Belinda. At night he would guard the girl faithfully to the door of her home, but never—no, not even if Belinda in play invited him thereto—would cross the threshold. If it were possible for the quality of self-respect to exist in a dog's heart, one would say this gaunt, forsaken, Spanish hound possessed it.

Self-respect, gratitude, love! I seem to be making a tolerable long list of Costa's virtues; but he had vices enough to counterbalance them. Society generally looked upon him as an abandoned thievish reprobate, and with good reason. Society always has good reason for its condemnatory verdicts.

How could it be otherwise? How could Costa, supperless, houseless, live the decent Philistine life that had been so easy to him in the well-fed days of the hidalgo, his master?

As long as Belinda's funds lasted he ate meat; when these failed he had such crusts and scraps as the girl could save from her own meals and carry away, unseen by Miss Burke, in her pocket. But scraps and crusts were not enough for Costa's sustenance. He must be dishonest or die; and (some Christians have felt the same) he preferred being dishonest.

In his youth he had been trained as a sporting dog, and, in all the pride of untempted virtue, had held by the code of honour of his peers, the arbitrary code which brands the slaughter of a barn-door fowl with indelible disgrace. But with other times other manners. If nobility oblige, how much more so does an empty stomach! Some lingering scruples, some remnants of the old finer sentiment, Costa had to get over; at first would only scare his victims, next pursue them, but not kill. At last, one autumn twilight—hunger sharp, Belinda, I regret to say, witness of the crime—he murdered a fat old hen asleep upon her roost, devoured, enjoyed her to her very feathers, and murdered conscience with the act.

The downward path lay smooth before Costa now. No man, it is remarked, becomes so finished a scamp as your scamp who was a gentleman once. The rule is not without its parallel as regards the demoralisation of dogs. Where an ordinary cur would have committed his highway thefts or murders in a gross sort of bungling way, certain of instant detection, Costa, aided by a hundred remembrances of his old greenwood craft, got through the work like an artist. He became "suspect," as you may imagine. Not a housewife within a couple of miles of St. Jean de Luz, but knew him by sight or by reputation. And still he lived. These southern people combine with the most absolute callousness as to animal suffering a curious superstition as to taking animal life. They will see a starving dog die, inch by inch, rather than knock him on the head ; will bury an obnoxious cat alive, not hang her. Costa lived—a disreputable, idle, lawless existence enough—but with fidelity, love, gratitude to the little girl who had saved him, ever strengthening.

So different of its kind is the deterioration of dog nature to that of man.

When Belinda was out late at night, as too often happened, Costa, with the strength and will to pull down half-a-dozen Carlists at a time, would keep sentry by her side ; when she was playing paume amongst her not too gentle comrades, would sit, winking his eyes with an air of dignified superiority in the shade, not interesting himself in the frivolous details of the game, but ready at any time, should dispute arise, to put himself forward as judge and executor of the law on Belinda's side. He knew when the child was glad or sorry, rich or poor. He knew her enemies, knew her friends; and from the first moment of meeting till the present one had cast ugly looks at the calves of Augustus Jones's legs.

"Try not to be frightened, Mr. Jones," says Belinda, glancing maliciously at the expression of her admirer's face. " Perhaps he won't bite, if you keep very quiet. Dogs know so well when people are afraid of them ! Have you come for macaroons, my old Costa, eh ? You have, have you ? Mr. Jones, Costa says he has come for macaroons." It may be observed that Belinda has not a grain of false pride on the score of begging alms for her friends. "Costa has come for macaroons, and I have not a single sou left in the world."

She stoops down, and with one arm bent fondly round the old dog's neck, looks up, with the prettiest beseeching air imaginable, at Augustus Jones. But Jones buttons up his pockets. He is not altogether a miser, as different sections of the London world have practically learnt ; will spend money freely enough on riding horses, bracelets, opera-stalls, churches that need showy windows, philanthropic effort that publishes printed lists; on his vices, his virtues, *his* anything. But macaroons for a dog! This absolute waste, this simple flinging of money, for the sake of flinging it, into the sea, Mr. Jones cannot stand. Looking upon the folly as a speculative investment, means to a possible end, 'twere different. "You desire to marry yourself, as you consider, well," could some voice whisper to him; "the ambition of your heart has been ever to wed your gold to aristocratic blood, and despairing of better chances you would fain win this out-at-elbows little Arab, the grand-daughter of the great Earl of Liskeard, for your wife. Humour her whims, even this present babyish one, if you would hope to succeed." Could Mr. Jones realise this as truth, the macaroons were Costa's. But he does not realise it. He is devoid alike of sympathy and of tact: qualities, both of them springing from imagination, not reason; and goes no further than his own light illumines the path. He detests all dogs, detests Costa in particular, with the bitterest of hatred, that which springs from fear. And, as I have said, Mr. Jones buttons up his pockets.

"Macaroons for Costa!" repeats Belinda, stretching out to him a little suppliant sunburnt palm. "Not like them? You should see whether he likes them! Try the experiment. Why, when Maria José was here we gave him two francs' worth all at once, and he ate them up before you could say Jack Robinson."

"Did he indeed?" says Augustus, looking disgusted, whether at the allusion to a rival or at the vulgarity of Belinda's speech, who shall say? "Then the only thing I can remark is, I am sorry Mr. Maria José had not better sense than to waste his money on such absurdity."

Quitting her hold on Costa, Belinda starts to her feet, and stands, upright and determined, before Augustus; her small child's face flaming red as any pomegranate flower.

"Mr. Jones," she exclaims, "if I asked you to give Costa two francs' worth of macaroons at this moment, do you mean to tell me you would not do it?"

"I should prefer giving the money to the first worthy object of commiseration who happened to pass along the street," Mr. Jones answers, didactically.

"Will you give Costa one franc's worth of macaroons, now, this instant?"

"I—I never heard of feeding a dog on macaroons. I think it a deuced ridiculous waste of money," stutters Jones, without offering to put his hand into his pocket. "I can be as liberal as most people, Miss Belinda, on the right occasion, but if I *have* a predilection, and a very strong one too, it's against seeing good money wasted."

Belinda looks at him, from his mosquito-bitten forehead down to the tips of his Bond Street boots; looks at him, with those clear eyes of hers, not only up and down bodily, but morally, through and through.

"Oh! I understand. I know now why Costa hated you from the first. Dogs are not such fools. If you *have* a predilection, you say 'tis against seeing good money wasted. If I *have* a predilection, and a very strong one, too, 'tis for wasting it. Money—bah! what is money? So many dirty bits of silver stamped with this head or that, and good just for the quantity of sweetstuff it will bring you. To spend, to waste, to scatter money to the winds, is one of my predilections; paume playing, bolero dancing— liberty, sweet liberty!—are the others! And I am no more likely to change in my opinions than you are in yours. Good-bye, Mr. Jones."

She turns on her heel, and swinging her schistera to and fro, in a way to shock Mr. Jones's nicest susceptibilities, walks off; Costa, his head well erect, as though he felt himself master of the situation, at her side.

CHAPTER III.

LIGHT WEDDED, LIGHT WIDOWED.

ST. JEAN DE LUZ is awakened from its afternoon siesta. By the time that the Paris train arrives, an hour later, every nook, every corner of the quaint little Basque town is full of life and colour. Castilian nurses, in the gay scarlet bodices and silver buttons of their order, are airing olive-faced babies in the Place; water-sellers, with their sing-song "*Agua! quien quieri agua?*" throng the streets; men smoking their final cigaritto before dinner, are to be seen under the awnings of the different cafés. The younger women are ogling from behind their fans, the old ones resuming their eternal tresillo on the balconies. Smoking, flirting, and card-playing—in short, the three great occupations of Spanish life—going on actively. And St. Jean de Luz, at the height of its brief bathing season, is as completely Spanish as any town in the Peninsula, the natives vanishing like mice into cellars and attics the moment good Spanish dollars can be got in exchange for their first and second floors.

As six o'clock strikes, a carriage draws up, with the extra flourishing of whips indicative of new arrivals to be fleeced, before the Grand Hotel Isabella. Waiters, chambermaids, mine host himself, all come out, salaaming, to secure their

prey, and forth steps an elegant fool of the very first water—
English, and of the sex whose helplessness is its charm—
upon the pavement. A clothes-artist might know that this
fair being is dressed in what the craft have agreed to call
"slight mourning." To the unprofessional eye, her attire,
a cunningly blent mixture of white and lilac, is suggestive of
no other grief than the despairing envy of every woman who
may chance to behold it, and the absolute collapse and
annihilation of man.

"*Mes baggages—où est mes baggages?*" sighs a voice, in
that curious language known as French in suburban boarding-schools, but unintelligble south of the Channel. "*Dix
baggages, tout adressé*, and a piece of blue ribbon on each.
Dix—ten—oh! *would* anybody make them understand?
Dix"—holding up ten helpless, lavender-gloved fingers.
"Really, Spencer, I think you might try to be of some little
use."

At this appeal, another elegant fool—but of second
water; a cheap copy of the first: flimsy glacé silk instead
of richest cord—steps languidly forth from the carriage.
She too is admirably helpless, and she too speaks a tongue
incomprehensible out of England—the polyglot smatter of
advertising Abigails who "talk three languages with ease,
and are willing to undertake any duties, not menial, while
on the Continent."

They address themselves to the host, to the waiters, to
the coachman. Nobody understands them; they understand nobody.

"If I had only bespoken Belinda!" sighs the lady
piteously. "If you had had the slightest consideration,
Spencer, you might have reminded me to telegraph to Miss
O'Shea."

The words have scarcely left her lips, when a knot of
little lads, English and French, shoulder their way along
the street—lads from about eleven to fourteen, sunburnt,

dare-devil looking young Arabs enough, bare-footed most of them, and with schisteras in hand. At the word "Belinda," the foremost of the gang turns, and nudges the boy who comes next. They all stop, they all stare; one of them gives a low meaning whistle across his shoulder, and in another second or two Belinda appears upon the scene, her battered hat more battered than when we first saw her two hours ago, the flush of heat and victory on her brow, her espadrilles so kicked to pieces, that how they keep upon her feet at all is miraculous—Belinda, like her associates, schistera in hand, with Costa, who has been rolling in the dust, and has a more disreputable look than usual, at her heels. She passes along, whistling, forgetful of Mr. Jones and their quarrel, of Rose's letter and threatened arrival—forgetful of everything except the game of paume she has just played and won—when suddenly our elegant fool, number one, looks full into the girl's face, and, electrified, recognizes her.

"What, Belinda?—can that be you?"
"What, Rose?—arrived already?"
"How dirty she is!" (mentally).
"How painted she is!" (all but aloud).

And then the ladies kiss, hugely to the entertainment of Belinda's comrades, who have certainly never before beheld Miss O'Shea engaged in any of these feminine amenities.

"You—you have grown, I think," says Rose, scrutinising, with horror-stricken eyes, the girl's ragged, dust-stained clothes, and remembering, with all the shame of which her small soul is capable, that the lady's maid scrutinises them also. "And you are sunburnt—you are very sunburnt, Belinda."

"I should say I was, just! If you had been playing paume under such a sun as this, you would be sunburnt too. But where is your maid? You don't mean to say you have travelled all the way from Brompton to St. Jean de Luz alone?"

Rose on this gives a side glance at her gorgeous Abigail, and whispers in Belinda's ear: "That is my maid, my dear, and the most helpless, the most unbearable creature in the world; still, as I had her from Lady Harriet Howes—and a particular favour her ladyship made of it—I don't like to change. It's an immense thing" (plaintively) "for one's maid to have lived in a *good style* of place, you know."

"I know!" repeats Belinda, with her mocking, gamin laugh. "Yes, I am just the fellow to know about fine ladies and their maids, am I not? But do you mean to say, Rose, that you and that magnificently dressed young woman have travelled from one end of France to the other without getting run away with?"

"I—I have not been altogether without an escort," responds the widow, and blushes.

Belinda thinks she must have been wrong about the paint, not knowing that there are women who blush and paint too.

"I was fortunate enough in Paris to come across a very old and dear friend, who took me about a little, and then, somehow or another, I met with him again at Bordeaux. Curious coincidence, was it not?" laying her plump hand with girlish playfulness upon Belinda's slender arm. "But I have more curious things to tell you when we are alone. *Mes baggages.*" This is to the dignified Basque coachman, who with the air of a prince, his cap on his head, stands waiting to be paid. "Belinda, will you make that savage comprehend that I want my luggage? I'm sure," says Rose, "my French must be better than most people's, for I had the prize two halfs following at Miss Ingram's. Poor mamma cried, I had worked myself to such a shadow. But the French speak with such an extraordinary accent, there's really no understanding them. Ten large boxes, tell him, each with a blue ribbon; and—oh, the awful dog! Some one take the awful dog away!" Costa has been critically examining the new comers, mistress and maid, and conveys his poor opinion of them to Belinda by a short, gruff bark. I thought all the dogs in France had to be muzzled by law. Spencer—Spencer! Get between me and that *monster!*"

It is long before Rose can be made to believe that her precious boxes will be brought from the station, like all other people's boxes, on the hotel omnibus. Then, when rooms have to be selected for her, arise new troubles. She must have a bed-room communicating with a drawing-room (and the drawing-room must have a balcony *covered* with flowers), a bed-room near some one else's in case of fire; a bed-room not too near some one else's in case of his talking in his sleep; and Spencer must be on the same floor; and is there any way of ascertaining who slept in the rooms last? Will Belinda request the people of the house to swear that there has been no one here with smallpox this summer?

"Swear? Why a Basque will swear anything you ask him," cries the girl, mischievously. "Of course, people with smallpox have slept here this summer, as they have at every hotel in the place. What does it matter, Rose? You will be so mosquito-bitten, like our friend Augustus, by to-morrow morning, that you won't recognize yourself in the glass. A touch of smallpox, more or less, cannot matter."

With which scanty consolation Rose, the tears rising in her foolish frightened eyes, has to be contented.

"If I only knew where all these dreadful doors lead to," she sighs, looking round her with pretty timidity as soon as Mrs. Spencer, her nose well in the air, has retired to inspect her own apartments. "But I have heard such stories of what goes on in foreign hotels—it was all in the papers, once, 'Judas doors,' I think they called them, and indeed the way Frenchmen stare at one in the street is enough. I declare nothing would ever tempt me to go out on the Continent alone."

She languishes away to a mirror, and taking off her veil begins to dust her delicate rose-and-white face with her cambric handkerchief. I use the words "dust" intentionally. Belinda, under the same circumstances, would rub her sun-tanned skin as vigorously as a housemaid rubs mahogany. But women of fashion have complexions, not skins. Rose treats hers fearfully, tenderly; as you will see a connoisseur treat the surface of some fine enamel, or other piece of perishable art, not, it may be, without reason.

"I have grown quite an old woman, have I not?" She puts a smile on the corners of her lips, then turns and presents her face for the girl's admiration. "I daresay you would hardly have known me if you had met me, without warning in the street? Now tell me the honest truth, dear; I hate flattery."

Rose, at this present time of her mortal life, has approached, as near as it is possible for a good-looking woman ever to do, to her fortieth year. But, if there be truth in that delightful French adage, that a woman is the age she looks, we may call her nine-and-twenty: of course I mean after her art-labours are over for the day.

"Few sorrows hath she of her own," this comely, silver-tongued, bewitching widow, and no sorrows of others could by any possibility make her grieve. So she is without wrinkles. The lines in which strong love, strong grief, strong feelings of any kind grave their story on human faces are all absent from hers. Round cheeks, breaking into dimples, like a baby's, when she smiles; wide-open eyes, of that unchanging yellow-hazel that often accompanies flaxen lashes and eyebrows; the most charming, most insignificant little nose you ever saw, and a mouth, not altogether good-tempered by nature, perhaps, but trained to every artificial "sweetness" of smile and word—such is Rose. Her hair, that once was palest hempen, is now as auriferous a copper as Bond Street chemistry can make it, and a marvel of luxuriance—such exquisite plaits and tresses, such sly-nestling unexpected little ringlets! (Has Belinda forgotten the old dinnerless days when her tired fingers had to crimp and plait and curl in the shabby London lodgings?) Her figure is plump, would be over plump, but for the corset-maker's torturing aid, and Rose's heroic resolve *never* to own a waist of more than twenty-two inches. Her complexion, fair naturally, improved by art, is —well, a complexion, not a skin. Need I say more?

Belinda examines her with eyes that would pierce all the enamel, all the rice-powder, in the world. "We none of us get younger, Rose; you no more than other people. But you look well in health. I am surprised to see you out of mourning," she adds, giving a cold glance at her stepmother's white and lilac finery. "Has your Uncle Robert been dead six, or eight weeks? I do not remember, exactly."

"Eight weeks! Oh, Belinda, dear, how thoughtless you are!" Rose, to do her justice, feels far more amiably disposed towards Belinda than Belinda feels towards Rose. Life flows at its smoothest, just at present, with Cornelius O'Shea's widow. Dear Uncle Robert opportunely removed to a better world; his will all that could be desired by surviving relatives: good looks within the reach of one's own industry still, and a lover, handsome, young, well-born, to crown all. How can Rose feel anything but amiable, especially now that she sees how unfortunately plain this poor little alien stepdaughter of hers has grown up? "Uncle Robert has been dead more than three months, and I am only just in second mourning. The milliners tell me it's ridiculously deep, and indeed I remember seeing

Lady Harriet wear scarlet less than six weeks after old Miss Howe's death, but I—I know *what* a friend I have lost! Of course I could not enter upon these delicate subjects in a letter, Belinda, but Uncle Robert has left me everything, unconditionally. Money, house, plate—everything. I only hope I may be guided" says Rose, turning up her eyes, "guided to make a right use of what is entrusted to me."

Colder and harder grows the expression of Belinda's face. Can the girl forget by whose absence, whose death, Rose's good fortune was purchased?

"Oh, you are very lucky, Rose, very! But somehow I cannot find words just now to wish you joy. What are your future plans? Are you going to live in that big house at Brompton all alone?"

Mrs. O'Shea's eyes sink to the ground. "I—I have many things to talk to you about, Belinda, as I hinted in my letter. But when I have told all my little story I am sure you will *feel for me* in my position. The romance of two young lives!" murmurs Rose, modestly apologetic. "Love sacrificed to duty—a heart slowly breaking during a dozen years! Belinda, my dear girl, you have heard . . . you must have heard of Roger Temple?"

But not by a word or look will Belinda assist the widow's bashfulness, or help her forward in her confession.

"I believe that I have heard of such a person, somewhere," she answers, in a tone of the most freezing indifference. "Your friend Mr. Jones mentioned him, I think, Rose. But I pay so little attention to anything Mr. Jones says."

"Belinda, when we were both young—the day will come, I hope, child, when you will sympathize more with the trials and temptations of others—when we were both young, Roger Temple and I first met. And he cared for me."

Dead silence: the widow confused, and stroking down the folds of her silk dress with her white fingers; Belinda's slip of a figure standing upright beside the window, her arms folded, her lips and eyes about as "sympathetic" as though they had been carved in granite.

"He cared for me—too much for his own peace—but duty stood between us, and we parted." Of this the reader shall know more than by Rosy's hazy utterances. "We parted. Fate was hard upon us both. And now . . . Belinda, must I say more?"

"Say everything, please, if you want me to understand you."

"Roger Temple has asked me to be his wife at last, and I——"

"And you are going to be married again!" interrupts Belinda, cruelly. "For the Third time! Then all I can remark is, you are very fond of being married, Rose."

A heartless, unwomanly speech enough; but Belinda, like many other raw girls of her age, is absolutely heartless in matters of love; and at this moment passionate unreasoning jealousy against the rival of her dead father is sending the blood to her brain too quickly for her to be very nice in the choice of words.

"I'm sure I don't know how you can be so unfeeling," says Rose, almost crying. "But you were always the same. Even when you were little you had no more sensibility than a stone. And Roger expresses himself so beautifully about your welfare, and the Temples are such a good family, and everything—and then to say that I—I of all women living—am fond of being married! I do hope, Belinda, whatever your own opinions may be, you will not wound me in this most heartless and indelicate manner before Captain Temple."

"Captain Temple!" repeats Belinda, all innocence. "Why, when am I ever likely to see Captain Temple?"

"You will see him here, in St. Jean de Luz, to-day."

"Captain Temple in St. Jean de Luz! You mean to tell me, Rose, that you *and a young man* are travelling about the world together?"

And Belinda, the first and last time in her life such hypocrisy can be recorded of her, puts on an air of outraged virtue edifying to behold.

"Roger met me in Paris and again in Bordeaux," says poor Rose, blushing through her rouge with vexation. "Roger was the old friend I told you of. And there was always Spencer . . . and we have taken care never to stop at the same hotel, even. He has gone now to look at a lodging in quite another part of the town. If you knew, Belinda, if you knew what a soul of honour Roger Temple has, you would not talk so lightly!"

"Ah, but you must remember I know nothing about him," retorts the girl, "and my education does not dispose me to take any man's honour on trust. Never mind, Rose," she goes on, with an assumption of pitying complaisance. "I am shocked, I own, but I will keep what I think to myself. I will not say a word, even to Burke."

"And you will behave with feeling, with consideration, to Roger Temple for my sake?"

Before the girl can answer, a man's step sounds in the corridor, a knock comes at the door.

"Entrez," cries out Belinda, in her clear young voice.

"My things!" sighs the widow, all in a tremor, her heart reverting to the possessions which lie nearer to it even than her lover—her bandboxes.

And the door opens.

"Roger! You have found your way already then?" Rose exclaims, with rather a forced little laugh, and retreating hastily from the light that falls unbecomingly full upon her through the open window. "Belinda, dearest, my very old acquaintance, Captain Temple. Now mind," with infantine candour, " I shall never forgive either of you if you don't fall in love with each other *at once*. I have been like that always—Miss Ingram used to say I was quite absurd. Whoever I am fond of must be fond of all my friends."

But long before Rose has ceased twittering her small falsities, Belinda's eyes and Roger Temple's have met—met and spoken the truth.

" In life as on railways," a master-hand has written " at certain points, whether you know it or not, there is but an inch, this way or that, into what train you are shunted."

Into what train has Belinda's passionate heart been shunted, all unknowing, at this moment?

CHAPTER IV.

WHAT MEN CALL LOVE.

ROSE spoke of the romance of two young lives, of love sacrificed to duty, of a heart slowly breaking during a dozen years. This may be set down as the poetic form of the story about herself and Roger. Now let us have it in the prose.

And in the first place I would remark, that if Roger Temple's heart had been breaking during the length of time Rose imagines, either it must have been an extraordinarily tough heart when first the process was set up, or the process itself is one that slightly affects a man's outward strength and health. He is a well-knit, handsome-looking fellow ; a little sallow, perhaps, like most men whose digestions have been too long tried by climate and curry, and with a touch of Indian listlessness in his English honest blue eyes. But as to heartbreak—wasting in despair—moral dyspepsia of any kind !—ask his brother officers, the comrades who know him best, what man in the regiment they would consider the most absolutely free from all such disorders, and ten to one the answer will be, "Roger Temple." A first-rate shot, a bold rider, a capital fellow at the bivouac or mess-table— these are the things you will hear respecting Roger among men. And as regards softer matters ? Oh, well, flirtation and young ladies are not very much in old Roger's line. If marriage is fated to overtake him, if the best fellow on earth is fated to be spoilt, it will have to be done by a *coup de main*. Roger might not have the heart to say no to a very pretty woman, if she asked him outright to marry her; but he would certainly never have energy to undertake the preliminaries of courtship himself.

Thus the coarse, indiscriminative voice of his fellow-men. How account for the discrepancy?

You remember Holmes's fancy as to three distinct personalities to be found in every man? First, the man himself, the real veritable Thomas. Second, Thomas's ideal Thomas. Third, the ideal Thomas of Thomas's friends. To these I would add, the ideal Thomas of Thomas's mistress; a man in love, judged with a woman's power of judging, from a woman's stand-point, being a human being as totally strange to the poor fellow's male friends and acquaintance as to his own consciousness.

The story, in the prose form, is simply this. Rose, married in her girlhood to an elderly London lawyer (with whom, as an absolute nonentity, the conventional husband of a charming wife, this little history has no concern)—Rose, early married, and launched into a narrow circle of dull professional respectability, was, at six and twenty, as really fresh and ingenuous a young person as ever breathed. Neither perruquier nor Bond Street chemist needed then. Her flaxen hair, smoothly braided according to the fashion of the day, adorned her youthful face. Her complexion, innocent of cosmetics, was, in spite of some few freckles, like a just opened dog-rose. Same order of intellect, same depth of heart as now; no knowledge of the world, save of her own little Pharisaical Bloomsbury Square world; small scope for vanity, less for sentiment. So Roger Temple met and loved her.

The Indian Mutiny was just over at that time, and Roger,

a fair-faced boy of nineteen, had come back wounded, after his first dark taste of soldier's work, to England. He made Rose Shelmadeane's acquaintance at an East London dinner-party, to which a family lawyer of the Temples, or other unimportant agent, had led him; made her acquaintance, sat opposite to her at table, and, not knowing till dessert, at least, that she was the crown and blessing of another man's life already, conceived for her as wild a passion as ever foolish lad conceived for still more foolish woman since the world began.

The London season was at its height; even Rose's humdrum life enlivened by an unwonted share of parties, theatre-going, drives in the park, visits to the Zoological—country cousins, who must be amused, staying in the house. Roger saw her, dogged her, worshipped her, everywhere. One of the country cousins being female and unmarried, it might be assumed that Mr. Temple's attentions were honourably matrimonial. Mr. Temple being well-born, young, handsome, of good expectations, was it not a manifest duty to afford him encouragement?

Thus Rose, with small platitudes, stifled her small conscience for a fortnight or so. Then the end came; the end to the prologue, not the play.

Watching the hippopotamus together one July Sunday afternoon at the Zoological, the country cousins, the nonentity of a husband, all but within earshot, young Master Roger made a fool of himself; in stammering passionate whispers told Mrs. Shelmadeane a secret which Mrs. Shelmadeane had been calmly aware of for some time past, but which it was shocking—oh, unendurably shocking!—even to think of, the moment the confession happened to find its way into words.

She walked away from him, her fair young matron face ablaze, and with the air of a new Cornelia, laid her hand upon her husband's arm. Three evenings later, Rose—twenty-six, remember, Roger nineteen—was waltzing with him at a ball, to which duty bade her chaperon her country cousins, at the Hanover Square Rooms.

Mr. Temple had been wicked—so wicked that it really took one's breath away to think of it—in daring to regard her, an honoured wife, save with the feelings of iciest respect and esteem. But then Rose, gentle soul, felt constrained to pity the poor misguided fellow—to lead him, if it might be, into better ways. And that Bloomsbury Square life and husband of hers, illumined by present experience, were so hideously monotonous; and the homage of a man, handsome, young, distinguished, like Roger, were so honey-sweet to vanity. And then think how the papers had spoken of Mr. Temple's bravery in India; think of all the horrid Sepoys he must have killed, his arm still in that interesting black sling! What could Rose do but accord the lad the friendship for which he pleaded, and agree to forget that fatal, erring, not altogether charmless moment, when they watched the hippopotamus together at the Zoo?

A better woman, or a worse one, a woman inspired by imagination or guided by experience, might have been terrified at such a position. Good, passionless, unimaginative, self-saturated Rose, the first little cold shock of the plunge over, felt no terror at all. What she did feel strongest, I think (when one can disinter it, sufficiently for analysis, from the mass of small vanities, triumphs before partnerless country cousins, et cetera, in which it was embedded), was —gratified sense of power.

"Scratch a slave's skin, you find a tyrant underneath." Rose, like some other millions of her sisters, had been a slave from her birth, first as a girl then as a wife—I speak of moral servitude, of course. All at once she found herself in the position of a ruler; and she used her new prerogative as human beings who are not to power born are apt to use it.

The young fellow gave up for her his time, his friends,

his pleasures; gave up for her his life; and received in return—what? Sermons, a soiled white glove or two, and enough half-dead flowers—he has some of these in his possession still—to fill a respectable herbarium.

By degrees the story got known, not in Rose's starched Bloomsbury Square circle, but among Roger Temple's bachelor friends, most of whom, indeed, contrived to gain a glimpse of Mrs. Shelmadeane. Heavens! what a commonplace dowdy little mortal poor Roger's divinity was pronounced to be by men not, like himself under the glamour of passion! Pretty, if you will; the kind of red-and-white stupid beauty you will meet a dozen times a day in any provincial town; but nothing, positively nothing, more. And Roger of all others, with his fastidious tastes, his high-flown boyish ideal of feminine grace and refinement, to have lost his senses about this little Bloomsbury Square prude! Roger, to whom half the best houses in town stood open, upon whom good and handsome and well-born women by the score would have smiled, had he so chosen!

The infatuation lasted out the London season. Then old Shelmadeane carried his wife off to Margate, tardily suspicious, perhaps, as to the kind of sacrifice she was making to duty, and Roger's leave of absence came to an end. He was angry, bitter, sick of heart; his divinity, during their last interview, having sermonised and sympathised, and altogether tortured him beyond measure; determined to return to India without seeing her again, determined to despise, to forget her. He determined all this; likelier than not, would have carried it into execution to the letter—at nineteen so much is possible to the human heart—had Mrs. Shelmadeane been willing. But Mrs. Shelmadeane was very far indeed from willing.

She was (I make the statement advisedly, unconditionally, so as not to go over the same ground again), both now and hereafter, one of the most rigidly virtuous women, as far as conduct goes, that ever breathed. She was not, certainly, at that early period of her life in any ordinary sense of the word, a coquette. But she loved her new taste of power with all the faculties for loving nature had bestowed upon her; and for no consideration, short of saving her soul from actual transgression, would have given her slave back his freedom. He must look forward to nothing; not even to the day when he might legitimately claim her hand. She would feel herself—oh, dear! the guiltiest of creatures if she could encourage anybody to look forward with hope to anybody else's death. What is such hope, Rosie would say, piously shaking her blonde head, but another kind of murder? Mr. Temple must look forward to nothing in the future, must ask for nothing in the present; must always remember, please, that she was married to a man whose *moral worth* she respected, always speak and act as if Mr. Shelmadeane were present. But whether he remained in England, or whether he went back to India, Roger Temple must not regain his freedom.

She wrapped up her feelings, even to her own soul, in the very prettiest tinsel-paper of all hypocrisy's store. To let that poor boy depart in his present frame of mind would be to let him depart desperate. He might even go and marry some Dreadful Creature, in revenge, as men with blighted affections have been known to do, and she would have the burthen on her conscience. Who should say what effect a perfect reconciliation, a few solemn sisterly words at parting, might have upon all the poor young fellow's future career?

And she wrote to him, a sweet little plaintive kind of note, in her school-girl hand, with her school-girl phrases—that, also, Roger Temple keeps still!

Accidentally Mr. Shelmadeane had heard in the City that Mr. Roger Temple was going back to India at once. Surely he did not mean to start without bidding his sincerest friends and well-wishers adieu? They had gone to Margate for change, and Margate was rather dull, Rosie confessed ingenuously; but Mr. Shelmadeane, on the whole, complained less of his gout, so she must be grateful. And they dined at six. And Mr. Shelmadeane was always at home, except on Mondays and Tuesdays. When would Mr. Temple come?

Neither on a Monday nor a Tuesday, as some older men, versed in the world's ways, might, after the receipt of such a note, have ventured upon doing. For no personal gratification would young Roger have abused the angelic, child-like simplicity of the woman he loved. Honourably, Quixotically, on a day when he was certain of finding the husband at home, he went down to Margate; and for the last time held Mrs. Shelmadeane's white hand in his.

What a parting scene it was to him! Dinner first—with the old lawyer prosing politics and grumbling over the dressing of his turbot, his wife with her girlish innocent face smiling nuptial smiles at him across the table. Then the dessert, torture of tortures, when Rosie insisted upon leaving her husband and "his" friend alone. Finally, the half hour's stroll on the beach, "just to smoke *one last* cigar with poor Mr. Shelmadeane," said Rosie, a tremor, discernible to Roger, if to no one else, in her soft voice. For about three minutes out of this half-hour, divinest, cruellest moments Roger's young life had experienced, chance willed that they should be alone; and in these their farewells were spoken— a madness of farewells, among the Margate bathing machines. And then old Shelmadeane pounced down upon them: "A quarter to nine, Sir. Unless you mean to miss your train, you must be off." And for a dozen shifting fateful years they saw each other's faces no more.

Long letters passed between them, with or without Mr. Shelmadeane's knowledge—I refrain from speaking with certainty on this point; but letters certainly that Mr. Shelmadeane, or any one else in the world, might have read with safety. Rosie, indeed, half thought, at times, that her victim repressed all allusion to his tortures too successfully. Every mail, every second mail, at first; then once in three or four months; then twice a year. So the correspondence attending Roger's ill-starred passion was carried on. At last Mr. Shelmadeane died.

And Roger Temple, of course, flew to England to put in first claim for the possession of his beloved one's hand? No! Roger Temple did nothing of the kind. He was away up the country, pig-sticking, when the letter containing the news of Rosie's widowhood reached him, after some delay. And he loved sport passionately; and the two or three men who formed the party happened to be his closest friends. And must not weeds be worn a decent time before they are replaced again by wedding favours? Considering Rosie's fine propriety of sentiment, her highly-strung shrinking nature, could a man dare . . . Well, 'twas a curious little imbroglio, altogether, highly illustrative of human weakness in the matter of attainable and unattainable desires. But our business at present being rather with the chronicling of fact than the dissection of feeling or motive, I proceed.

Roger neither rushed to England nor wrote any letter designed to compromise his Rosie's newly-gained liberty. It must be remembered that he had now been wasting in despair during a good many years; also that men get into the habit of everything, even hopeless passion, and, against their better reason, may feel disturbed by having to abandon a settled mode of thought. Like the proverbial Frenchman who exclaims, when, after a lifetime's separation, he is about to be lawfully united to the woman he loves, "But what shall I do with my evenings?" Roger Temple, on old Shelmadeane's death, might have been tempted to ask himself, "But what shall I do with my despair?"

"The greatest charm of a married woman," says a spiteful dramatist, "is invariably—her husband."

When Roger's foolish lips first stammered their secret in the Zoological Gardens, or trembled out their mad farewells upon the Margate beach, it would have been hard to convince him that Mrs. Shelmadeane's greatest charm was Mr. Shelmadeane. But time sharpens many an epigram that seems pointless to us in our youth.

He wrote the widow as exquisitely delicate a letter of condolence as was ever penned: putting himself, and his own selfish hopes and fears, utterly away in the background; dwelling only on her and on her loss. He spoke tenderly, but with vagueness, of the long years of their separation; he spoke, with greater vagueness still, of the day of their possible reunion. Of marriage, of anything that could by possibility be construed into a hint of marriage, he spoke not a word.

An ordinarily intelligent woman, before she read such a letter to the end, would have known that her lover's love for her was over. Rose, guided by the irrefragable logic of folly, deduced from it only a new proof of her slave's devotion.

"There is one, far distant, who adores me, but who is too high-souled, too generous, to think of anything but *my* grief!" she would say to Major O'Shea, who obtained an introduction to the pretty widow, and indeed set steadily to work love-making, before her crape was six weeks old. "Ah, Major O'Shea, if *you* had only the conscientiousness, the noble, forbearing, unselfish nature of that poor fellow in India!"

And then Cornelius would respond to the effect of his heart being stronger than his reason, of his impetuous feelings (he was nearer fifty than forty at the time, and had been in love, after one fashion or another, since he wore jackets), his impetuous feelings hurrying him beyond the cold bounds of conventional decorum. And the widow would sigh and blush and wipe a tear or two, and call him a sad, sad man, as she yielded her hand to be kissed. And the upshot of it all was, that the next news Roger Temple got of Rose Shelmadeane, was a flowery announcement in the *Times* of her infidelity to him—by special license, an archdeacon and three or four of the lesser clergy assisting, at St. George's, Hanover Square.

Singular perversity of men's nature! The news of this marriage cost him not only the most poignant jealousy, but a revival of his love in all its first fresh ardour. The existence of a husband, of any husband, seemed, really, some necessary mysterious condition of Roger Temple's passion. You should have seen the letter of good wishes that he wrote the bride; bitterest veiled reproach discernible through every courteous phrase, every pleasant little congratulatory message to Major O'Shea! Rosie cried herself almost plain for the day after receiving it, hid it jealously from Cornelius; to whose philosophic mind the whole matter, you may be sure, would have been one of profoundest indifference; and wrote Roger a pleading, self-extenuating reply by return of mail with three violets—ah, did Captain Temple remember the bunches of violets he used to bring her during the *happy days* of their friendship in Bloomsbury Square?—enclosed.

And Captain Temple, Rose has had his own word for it since, kissed the violets and letter both, and set up the writer on the old pedestal in his imagination—I was very nearly writing his heart—that she had ever held.

As Roger himself stands, hat in hand, all this time, awaiting Belinda's reception of him, we will have done in as few words as possible with retrospect of the love story. Some slight insight into Rose's domestic grievances, as Mrs. O'Shea, the reader has had already; we need not further enlarge upon them. Cornelius spent her money, neglected her, went to America, where his fate awaited him. And Rose, on her Uncle Robert's death, found herself once more free—free, and with a handsome little income, villa at Brompton, plate, linen and accessories at her own disposal.

And then it was that she and her old lover looked again upon each other's faces. Roger had returned to England unexpected by his friends, his long leave having been given him some months earlier than he anticipated; and on a certain May night, Rose at that moment believing him to be thousands of miles away in India, knocked at the door of the Brompton villa and inquired, in a voice whose accents he vainly strove to command, if Mrs. O'Shea was at home.

It was late for a visit of ceremony, between ten and eleven o'clock, and the starched-looking butler of occasion who answered his knock informed him pompously that Mrs. O'Shea was at home, but not visible to strangers. Mrs. O'Shea had had company to dinner, and——"

"Mrs. O'Shea will see me," interrupted Roger. "You need not even announce me. I am expected."

And in another minute he found himself among the wax-lights and guests and bran-new gilding and upholstery of Rose's drawing-room.

He slipped in, unannounced, as he desired, and looked round the assemblage in vain for Rose. Seven or eight women, of quasi-fashion, bare-shouldered, jewelled, flower-bedecked, were present. He looked among them in vain for the modest face and smoothly-braided blonde head of Rose Shelmadeane.

At last a fluffy-haired, brilliantly complexioned—alas, that I must write it!—middle-aged lady, came forward to him and bowed: a lady extremely overdrest, or undrest, as you like to term it. "I am not aware that I have the honour," she began, looking at him strangely.

And then he knew her voice.

Poor Rose, if she could have seen into her quondam lover's heart just at that moment!

He watched her, during the next hour or so, with feelings about equally balanced of disappointment and blank surprise.

Every woman's good looks must decline after the lapse of the twelve best years of her maturity, and Rose's had really, in the common acceptation of the phrase, "worn well." But it was not any fading due to age; it was not Time's natural footprints on cheek or brow that shocked him thus: it was the absolute startling *transformation* of her whole personality!

Soberest, most dove-like of young matrons at twenty-six, Rose, a dozen years later, had developed into the very friskiest of mature syrens, all her girlish promise of silliness ripened into a bounteous harvest of meridional folly. The lint-white smooth-braided locks were copper-gold now, frizzled high in wondrous monstrous pyramids above her head, with outlying curls and puffs and chignons that defy description. The faint rose bloom complexion had become definite pearl and carmine, the pale eyebrows grown dark; the eyes, not wholly innocent of belladonna, were a little fixed and hard, the decorous half-high dress of the old Bloomsbury Square days was replaced by—well, by the drapery of a Greek statue.

Roger, who had lived so long away from London, did not know that this is the received way in which the modern English matron of repute "grows old gracefully," and, as I said, gazed at poor Rose's full-blown charms with a sensation curiously blent of amazement and repulsion—a sensation, let me add, of which he was himself heartily ashamed.

This lasted till the departure of Rose's guests left them alone; then, hearing more of the old, sweet, appealing voice —no meretricious change had affected that—and his eyes, it may be, growing accustomed to the outward plastering of his ruined idol, Roger's heart got softer.

He had not really dined, Mrs. O'Shea discovered—had arrived in London late that afternoon, and forgetful of bodily sustenance, had rushed away to call on her at once. So a little supper was organised, accompanied by a bottle of Uncle Robert's best champagne. And then this man and woman, who had played at love so long, began, looking into each others eyes, to talk of all that they had suffered (in imagination or reality) since they parted; and the cruel intervening years faded away; they were whispering beside the hippopotamus; they were murmuring farewells upon the Margate beach again; and by and by Rose's hand, youthful and white still, found its way into Captain Temple's. It trembled; he pressed it to reassure her. Rose, with a sigh, made a feint of moving away, and then, for the first time in their lives, there lips met—and Roger's fate was sealed.

The wax lights had burnt low by now, and Rose kept her face well in shadow—nay, hid it bashfully out of sight on her lover's breast. And when he kissed her beautiful golden hair it never occurred to him to think from what dead head it might have been sheared; and when at last she lifted up her face to falter out softest promises of life-long truth, he did not even see the deposit of rice-powder it had left upon his waistcoat.

Who loves, cavils not; and Roger Temple, or Roger Temple's imagination, loved, during this hour's intoxication, at least.

What he thought and felt next morning, when he had to review his position and Mrs. O'Shea's complexion by daylight, none but Roger Temple ever knew.

He was not, it must be borne in mind, a ladies' man, had associated little with women during the later years of his life, had studied them but less; and his reverence for the whole sex was extreme, based rather on ideal foundations, indeed, than on fact. If sometimes the sense of his mistake galled him, if sometimes he felt the shame inseparable from the position of a lover who loves not, you may be sure that Rose and the world never found it out. Rosie loved him! What matters some disparity of years if a woman's affections be young? When the fruit after which a man has longed for years drops between his lips at last, has he a right to complain because time has somewhat over-mellowed its flavour?

So Roger would fain argue himself into good conceit with his bargain—so reconcile his heart to the attainment of its fondest desires.

And still, at times, his spirit is heavy laden; still, through rouge and bismuth and pearl-powder, old age *will* peer out at him from the face of his betrothed, and turn his heart cold.

"You really grow more and more foolish every day you live, my dear Roger!" Rose will remark, prettily conscious of her own charms, as she meets his gaze. "What can it be, I wonder, that makes you look at me as you do?"

"The years of our separation, my love," is invariably Roger's answer. "I have to make up now, remember, for the dozen years during which I never saw your face."

And Rose, promptly satisfied by any appeal to vanity, asks no more.

CHAPTER V.

COMPLIMENTS, NOT CARESSES.

BELINDA'S eyes have met Roger's, and, in spite of all her foregone jealous resolves, the girl finds it hard to steel herself against Rose's future husband. Never in her whole vagabond loveless life had such honest, human sunshine shone on her as shines now in Roger Temple's smile.

"I don't know about falling in love, but I am sure Belinda and I mean to be friends, Rosie," he says, advancing. "Do we not, my dear?"

And before Belinda can find time to put herself on guard, Captain Temple's bronzed moustache has touched her cheek. It is the kind of salutation that could scarce, by the very iciest prude, be stigmatised as a kiss, and yet it bears a sufficiently marked family resemblance to one to be unpleasant, exceedingly, in Rose's sight.

"I—I—really, Roger, Belinda looks so ridiculously younger than she is!"

"Not a bit," cries Roger; and now he rests his hand kindly on the little girl's shoulder. "Belinda is fifteen years old—you told me, did you not, that she was fifteen? Well, and she looks it. Don't mind Rosie, Belinda. Rosie turns rusty at the thought of having a grown-up daughter."

"I shall be seventeen the week after next," says Belinda,

holding up her chin. "I don't know what people mean by taking me for a child. I have certainly seen enough of the world and its wickedness to make me *feel* old," she adds, with the accustomed hard little rebellious ring in her voice.

"Belinda will look different—I trust Belinda will look totally different when she is properly dressed," says the widow, glancing down at her own elegantly flowing draperies. "I must really have a serious talk with Miss Burke about these short skirts."

"Ah! but Miss Burke is not here to be talked with, Rosie," cries Belinda, bent, it would seem, on disclosing every obnoxious truth she can hit upon. "My natural guardian and protector has been away in Spain a week or more, collecting facts for her book, and I am knocking about alone, as you see me—me and my dog Costa."

"Alone!" stammers Rose, shocked, not so much at the fact itself, as at having the fact exposed before Roger. "You don't mean actually alone, my dear?"

"Well, no; I have my chums, of course—the fellows who were with me in the street when you arrived. Now, Rose," she goes on pitilessly, "tell the truth. Were you, or were you not, ashamed when you first saw me?"

"I—I was surprised, Belinda," says Rose, in her sweetest little feminine treble. "It is not usual in England, you know, to see a girl of seventeen wearing her dress above her ankles; and then those fearful—what must I call them, Belinda? What do they call those fearful door-mat things you have on your feet?"

"They call those fearful things alpargatas in Spanish, espadrilles in French," answers Belinda, coolly holding out a ragged sandalled foot for inspection. "If you played paume on the hot sand for hours together as I do, you would be glad to wear espadrilles, Rose; yes, or to go bare-foot altogether, as I do, oftener than not."

A blush of burning shame rises over the widow's face.

She has made a good deal of small capital, one way or another, out of Belinda's high birth, to Roger, who is somewhat unduly sensitive about his future wife's connections, generally. The Earl of Liskeard's grand-daughter—so like all the Vansittart family—without being regularly pretty, a great air of breeding, of distinction, about our poor little Belinda, et cetera. And now to find her—what?—ragged, dirty, with the speech and manner (this is Rose's verdict, not mine) of a charity-school child, and mentioning, actually mentioning before a gentleman, the indelicate word " bare-foot."

"Our dear Belinda wants a year or two of sound English training," she remarks, in a tone that to Roger sounds dove-like, but that Belinda remembers and interprets only too well. "That is the worst of Continental education. One has to sacrifice so many solid English qualities for accomplishments. Still, in these days a girl *must* be accomplished. A couple of years in a select English boarding-school will, I have no doubt, render Belinda all that our fondest wishes could desire."

Belinda, on the conclusion of this little tirade, looks hard into her stepmother's eyes for a moment or two; then, shouldering her schistera, she moves across to the door.

" I must be off, Rosie," turning and bestowing a nod full of caustic meaning on the lovers. "And unless you want me to join some gang of wandering Gipsy players, as I have often thought of doing, you had better not talk about boarding-schools any more. My accomplishments, Captain Temple!" looking with an air of mock modesty at Roger. " Rose talks of my accomplishments, for which the 'good solid English qualities' have been sacrificed. I will tell you what they are, and you shall say which I am best suited for—a booth in a Basque fair or a select English boarding-school. Paume playing—'tis the same game, Mr. Jones tells me, as your English fives; paume," checking off each "accomplishment" on her dark slim fingers as she proceeds; "bolero-dancing; a tolerable acquaintance with slang in four languages——"

"Belinda!"

"Oh, let me finish the list, Rose! Let me make the best of myself that I can in Captain Temple's eyes. Bolero-dancing, slang, paume—of each a little. Knowledge, learnt practically, of how to keep myself and my dog on twenty sous a day board wages; and a taste for bull-fights so strong, oh, so strong!"—this with unaffected enthusiasm—"that I would sooner go without meat for a fortnight and church for a year, than miss the chance of going to one. For further particulars, apply to Mr. Augustus Jones."

And so exit Belinda, whistling, yes, Rose whistling!— keep from fainting if you can—as she goes.

"A quaint little original, our future daughter," says Roger, whose eyes have certainly opened wider during the conclusion of Belinda's tirade; "but a good-hearted child, I'll be bound. You must not be too hard on her, Rose."

"I hard!" sighs the widow, looking at him reproachfully. "When was I ever hard on any one? If you knew, Roger —but of course men never understand these things—the trial that poor girl has always been! I can assure you, I look upon Belinda as a Chastisement, sent to me for some wise purpose by Providence."

She seats herself on a sofa, discreetly away in the half-light, and with an air of resignation takes out her pocket-handkerchief. "I have made sacrifices no real mother would have made for her—can I ever forget the *devoted blind* attachment of her dear papa for me?—sending her away, Heaven knows at what expense, to the Continent, and always writing that she should have the best masters and everything; and now this is the result! How painfully plain she is!"

"Plain? No, Rosie, anything but plain. Belinda is just at that awkward age when one does not know what to make of girls, and her dress is not quite like other people's, is it? But she has magnificent eyes and a pretty hand ——"

"A pretty hand! Belinda's hands pretty! Why, they are enormous—six and three-quarters, at least, two sizes bigger than mine; and as brown! But you think every one you see lovely, Roger," says Rose, pettishly. "I declare one might just as well be ugly oneself. I have never heard you speak of any woman yet that you could not find something to admire in her——"

"And all because of you, my dearest!" cries Captain Temple, with warmth. "When a man admires one woman supremely, can you not imagine that every other woman— yes, even the plainest—must possess something fair in his sight, for her sake!"

He comes across to her, stoops, and rests his hand on his betrothed's fair head. It is a favourite action of Roger's, and one that Rose would be exceedingly well pleased to see him abandon. Who can tell what horrible trick postiche or plait may not play one in some unguarded moment of more than common tenderness?

"Oh, Roger, how can you?" She shifts a little uneasily from his touch. "Really, you get sillier and sillier every day." It is a fixed idea of the widow's that Roger Temple's feelings for her are precisely of the same irrepressible and rapturous nature as they were when he was a boy of nineteen; a happy fixed idea, lightening Roger's courtship more than he wots of. "Lucky, I am sure, that Belinda is gone. Do you know, I was so afraid you would say or do something *embarrassing* before her. How do I look, Roger, dear? Tired and hideous, don't I? Now, I insist upon your telling me the truth."

"How do I look, Roger, dear?" is the burden ever of their love scenes. Compliments, not caresses, are what Rose's heart of hearts yearns for; and Roger, after the past few weeks' apprenticeship, finds it no very difficult task to frame them. To have to pay compliments to the same woman during six or eight hours of every consecutive day would, in most cases, be a tolerably severe strain on a man's imaginative faculty. Rose, who is absolutely without imagination, herself, requires the exercise of none in others. A parrot gets no more wearied with it own eternal "Pretty Poll," than does poor Rosie of the eternal pointless stereotyped commonplaces of flattery.

"You look charming, Rose. I never saw you look better. Your eyes are as bright ——" Roger does not find a simile come readily to his hand, but Rose is content to take his good intentions on trust. "And your dress—all those lavender frills, and this white lace! Rosie, how is it that you always manage to wear prettier dresses than any other woman in the world?"

He must have asked her the same question, on a moderate calculation, about two hundred times since they were first engaged. At this moment he knows how often he has asked it, and the precise flutter of denial and little bewitching foolish laugh with which Rosie will respond. And he sighs; if he had courage to relieve his soul in the way nature prompted, would yawn. Terrible point in a love affair when we have learnt to disguise a yawn under a sigh! Terrible point in a love affair when we have learnt to disguise anything!

"I shall be quite unhappy about my dresses if they do not arrive soon," Rose goes on presently. "Ten large cases, you remember"—does not Roger remember those awful ten cases well—in Paris, Bordeaux, everywhere?—"and a bit of blue ribbon on each. There can be no mistake, if the railway people are honest, but abroad one never knows. I'm sure nothing would have been easier than for Belinda to run back to the station; still, she did not offer, and in my delicate position, as a stepmother, I have never required the slightest attention from the poor girl. Oh, Roger,"—Rose's

hand is in her lover's now, and he is beside her on the sofa
—"if I dared, how much I should like to tell you a secret,
something we are all concerned in ! "

Roger's natural reply is, what should prevent her telling
it ? Ought there to be any secret, present or to come,
between persons whose lives, like theirs, are to be spent in
one long delightful confidence ?

"Well, then—I'm a very naughty girl, I know," Rose
avows, kittenishly, " and I daresay you will scold me sadly ;
but I've been matchmaking. It is not quite by accident that
Mr. Augustus Jones is in St. Jean de Luz."

" Accident or no accident, the fact is a deuced unpleasant
one," remarks Captain Temple. "How or why Mr. Jones
came here is Mr. Jones's own concern ; but the bore of
having to encounter him! I really did hope, Rose, that we
had seen the last of that atrocious man when we left
London."

" You are prejudiced against him, Sir. I'm afraid you
don't like poor Augustus because he was a little too attentive
to me."

" Rose ! "

" Oh, come, Roger, I know what your ruling passion is,
and always has been. The green-eyed monster, Sir——"

" Rosie, I swear——"

" Well, we cannot help these things, my dear. I am
ridiculously without jealousy myself. Poor Major O'Shea
often said he wished he could see me a little *more* jealous,
but I can make every allowance for it in others. I ought, I
am sure," adds Rose, with a reminiscent sigh, " I ought to
bear all the jealous suspiciousness of men's natures after the
experience I have had."

There is silence for a minute, and anyone watching
Roger Temple's face attentively might discover there a good
deal the look of a man who is trying to repress his weariness
under the perpetual exacting babble of a child. "I don't

think you judge of me quite correctly, Rose," he remarks after a time. "Who ever judges another correctly? Who can read but by his own light? We were talking of Mr. Jones, were we not? Ah, yes. And you think me jealous of Jones? So be it, my dear. Poor little Rosie!" He bends forward and salutes the widow's cheek, tenderly, I may almost say, fearfully. Roger is better acquainted with feminine weakness, as regards rice-powder especially, than he was on that first fatal night at Brompton. "And now what about this grand secret of yours? You have been matchmaking, have you? I hope you don't mean to marry our little daughter Belinda to Mr. Augustus Jones?"

"He would be an extremely nice husband for her, from a worldly point of view," says Rose, turning over and over the diamond, a gift of Roger's, that rests on her plump third finger; "and as to education, old Mr. Jones was sensible of his own deficiencies, and had his son coached up by the most expensive tutors. Any one hearing Augustus talk would say that he was quite well educated enough, for a moneyed man."

"And presentable enough, refined enough?—the sort of husband a girl could not only love, but be proud of? Well, Rosie, manage it as you choose. If you like Mr. Jones, and if Belinda likes Mr. Jones, you may be sure I shall not forbid the banns."

"Ah! there is the difficulty. Belinda does not like Mr. Jones. Belinda and I have never liked the same thing or person yet." Poor Rosie! If the mantle of prophecy could but fall upon her shoulders at this moment! "But you could help me so much, dear, if you would—and you will, I know," upraising her eyes coaxingly to her lover's. "You will help me in my plans for Belinda's happiness? It was all through me, Roger, don't be cross with me if I confess the truth, it was all through me that Mr. Jones came to St. Jean de Luz."

"Through you that Mr. Jones came to St. Jean de Luz! And why should I be cross with you, you little goose?"

Rosie talks like a girl of sixteen; Roger treats her like a girl of sixteen; yet is sensible, mournfully sensible, ever, of the grotesqueness of so doing.

"You see, I knew that Augustus was anxious to marry. I suspected—feared," says Rose, with modest grace, "that his hopes *in some directions* might have been just a little blighted; and the thought struck me—as he was going abroad and had asked me to plan his tour for him—the thought struck me to bring him and Belinda together. What he wants is, connection; what she wants is, money——"

"But Belinda is a child still," interrupts Roger Temple. "You are building all these castles in the air, dear kind little soul that you are, Rosie, for her good; but the thing is ridiculous. Belinda's home must be with us for the next three or four years; ample time then to begin matchmaking. How could a child of her age possibly decide?" goes on honest Roger. "How could an innocent-hearted child of Belinda's age decide whether she ought or ought not to sell herself for the carriage-horses and diamonds of a snob like Jones?"

"Roger, my dear," answers Rosie, in her sweetest, most angelic tones—whenever she is annoyed, Mrs. O' Shea's angelic proclivities become more marked—"excuse me if I tell you that all those romantic ideas about 'selling oneself' are out of date. Belinda never was a child. Belinda has not one youthful sentiment belonging to her; and as to innocence, poor thing! you heard what she said about bull-fights. Do you think," says the widow, "I could go to a bull-fight without fainting? Those fine interesting-looking fellows in such danger, and the horrid bulls goring everybody! I'm sure, to see a picture, to read a description of one, is sickening enough."

"A matter of custom and nerve, Rosie. I have known

some Englishwomen capable of worse cruelty than being present at a bull-fight"

"And the very best thing for the girl's safety and our peace of mind will be to get her respectably settled as quickly as possible. My own opinion of Belinda—I would say so to no one but you, Roger—is, that she is without heart; and a woman without heart——"

But the generalisation is opportunely cut short by the arrival of the boxes and blue ribbons. In her joy over her recovered finery Rosie forgets all other human considerations; and her lover, with orders only to smoke one cigar, and to be back at the post of duty in an hour at latest, recovers a breathing space of liberty.

CHAPTER VI.

"MRS. GRUNDY, SIR!"

A PINEWOOD ball-room, wide open on three sides to the sea; an orchestra, composed of harp and piano; a second smaller room for écarté and tresillo—such is the San Jean de Luz Casino. Hither, evening after evening, resorts as motley a crowd as you will anywhere meet in your travels: the bluest blood of Castile side by side with Jew shop-keepers from Burgos; heads crowned and decrowned; wandering artists; respectabilities and other respectabilities —all jostled together in the delightful republicanism of watering-place life. Hither, when the absence of Miss Burke gives her freedom by night as well as by day, comes Belinda.

Not within the precincts, sacred to payers, of the ball-room. A terrace of sand extends round the whole area of the building, and from this terrace Belinda, with other waifs and strays like herself, is accustomed to watch the dancers, the dresses, the pretty women, the flirtations inside; I am afraid not without some occasional sharp pangs of envy at her heart.

Once, and once only, has the poor little girl been asked to dance. Maria José de Seballos, the beringed and bergamotted young Seville wine merchant, who, as we have seen, still holds a place in her dreams, did, on one never-to-be-forgotten evening, the last before he left St. Jean de Luz, invite her for a waltz. And Belinda, in her shabby dress and espadrilles, was, for the space of about eight minutes, in Paradise, whirling—blissfully whirling, among ladies in silks and flowers and jewels, the arm of a real grown-up partner supporting her, the whispers, sweet to vanity, though redolent of garlic to the senses, of a real grown-up partner in her ear.

Such a stroke of fortune, she knows, is not likely to befall her again. Maria José talked nonsense to her in plenty (such nonsense as men of all nations do talk when they dance with unfledged girls); bade her remember him in her prayers till the day came when he should return and carry her away for good to Seville, and so on. But Maria José, let Belinda dream as she may, is gone for ever. Mr. Jones, the only other young man she knows in the world, does not dance round dances, and certainly would not choose a partner in a black frock and frayed sandals if he did. Her lot in life is to look on, a wallflower not yet seventeen, with pulses beating madly to the music, and nimble feet that will not hold themselves still, and eyes that say, "Dance with me! dance with me!" to all the smart young gentlemen as they lounge up and down the ball-room; smart young gentlemen who, if they see Belinda at all, see in her only an ugly child in pigtails and a torn frock, and whose coldly indifferent glances her heart, older than her looks, is not slow to interpret.

She haunts the terrace, as is her wont, Costa at her heels, between nine and ten o'clock on this first evening of Rosie's arrival. It is an unusually gay little ball at the Casino; some near connection of ex-Spanish royalty present; and the dancing-room is thronged. Swan-like throats and delicate complexions from Madrid; Oriental eyes and Titian-ike colouring from Seville; marble whiteness and chiselled

Grecian features from Cadiz. Oh, what pretty women these Spaniards are! What a jest is life to them A song, a waltz, a flirtation in their earlier years, and then tresillo and prayers to the end. As responsible, examination-passing, degree-taking human creatures, women of Anglo-Saxon race have everything to be proud of—thankful for; but, knowing nothing, like children, and like children enjoying everything, how thoroughly, unconsciously charming are these soft-faced women of the South!

They are in full dress, almost without exception this evening. On occasions when a Parisian woman of fashion will drape her meagre charms to the chin, a Spanish one will invariably appear bravely bare-shouldered. And this not in the ball-room or on the balcony only. Of a moonlight night, here in St. Jean de Luz you will meet them by dozens, full dressed—yes, and in satin slippers, with flowers in their hair—calmly promenading along the streets or in the public gardens of the town. And what a becoming full dress it is! The national veil and high comb, à la manola, which a short time back were things well nigh of the past throughout the Peninsula, are the highest mode among the Spanish aristocracy to-day. So can the party whose motto is "*Fuera el estrangero*" mutely protest against the intruder now profaning the sacred throne of the Castiles. How fervently every painter must hope that no political revulsion will send these graceful malcontents back to the trailing skirts and towering head-gear and ever-changing milliners' modes, each one more inartistic than the last, of Paris and London!

"They are not exactly bad-looking," says Rose, glancing about her coldly; "not quite such an *orange* yellow as I expected. But their style is distressingly theatrical, is it not, Mr. Jones?"

Rosie has come to the Casino Ball well escorted; Mr. Jones, who is also staying at the Hotel Isabella, on one side;

her legitimate slave—I mean her future lord and master—on the other.

"Captain Temple," she runs on, to Roger; "you say you think these creatures handsome! How would you like to see any one you cared for, any Englishwoman, dance in public with a bare neck and a short skirt as they do?"

"The short skirts display admirable ankles, Rose," replies Roger. "Are introductions necessary in these parts of the world, I wonder? I should like to tempt my fate with that little blonde in pink satin, if I dared. Or will you waltz with me yourself, Rosie?" In a whisper, this. "For the sake of old days, my love. We have never waltzed together since that night—you remember it?—at the Hanover Square Rooms."

But Rosie, a good many years ago, gave up round dancing, finding that exercise, indeed, physically incompatible with the maintenance of a waist of twenty-two inches. She enforces her position now upon the very rigidest moral and æsthetic grounds.

"I never waltz, on principle, Roger. I do not approve of fast dances. I think it the worst possible taste for a woman who has experienced the serious sorrows of life to take part in such frivolity. But dance, pray, if you like. Think of your own amusement, not of mine. I understood that we came here to look on. But it does not matter. Nothing matters. Amuse yourself! I dare say Mr. Jones will not mind having to take care of me while you are away."

Tears are in Mrs. O'Shea's eyes; and Roger, of course, remains. It is no very great sacrifice for him to make. The little blonde in pink satin is distractingly pretty; she is glancing at him above her fan at this moment; but a man who has passed the dozen best years of his life in Madras can scarcely be enthusiastic about waltzing with the thermometer at ninety-eight. And it is better—a dozen times daily

Roger tells himself this—better far to get broken thoroughly and at once, to the bit which he has voluntarily taken between his teeth. A man choosing a bride of Rosie's age must learn to "look on" at most of life's amusements, and by her side. Poor Rosie! Would the dear little woman be as dear, as lovable, as thoroughly a woman as she is, if she possessed strength of mind sufficient to be devoid of jealousy? Is he not only too lucky a fellow to have won her, charming feminine weaknesses and all, as his own?

The dear little woman, though she will not accord the objectionable pleasure of waltzing to her lover, sees no evil in an occasional mild flirtation or two on her own account. Augustus Jones is her devoted attendant. Augustus introduces, ere long, some other young Britons, much of his own stamp, picked up at the table-d'hôte of the Hotel Isabella. Rose is "surrounded:" Frenchmen and Spaniards turning to look at the passée pretty Englishwoman, as she smiles and chirrups, and casts up her eyes with all the well-considered airs and graces of mature coquetry at her loud-talking young compatriots.

Roger takes himself quietly off among the crowd. Waltz he will not, as Rosie on such high grounds disapproves of waltzing; but, though his limbs be fettered, no embargo as yet is laid upon his eyesight. For a short time longer in this mortal life Roger Temple may at least, admire. He comes across the blonde in pink satin, whose eyes and fan make play at him as only the eyes and fan of a Spanish woman can; comes across other blondes, other brunettes. Finally he reaches the end of the room that stands open to the sea-shore, goes out for a breath of cooler air, probably not without dreams of a consolatory pipe under the starlight, and finds himself face to face with his future daughter.

"What, Belinda, my dear! Alone, in the dark and no partner? Let me take you to Rosie."

"Not if I know it, Sir! I come here to watch the amusements of my betters, not to show myself. Think of Rose's face of horror if I walked across the ball-room to her like this," holding out a fold of her ragged frock with a gesture in which there is to the full as much pride as humility.

"Rosie is far too kind-hearted to take notice of your dress," says Roger. "All Rosie cares for is to see other people happy."

"H'm! I see you are an excellent judge of character, Captain Temple."

"And then she could introduce you to partners—I take it for granted you like dancing? Rosie has got hold of some young men from the hotel, who would, I am sure, be only too happy——"

"To take pity on my forlorn condition if my mamma did her best to make them? Captain Temple, do you think, seriously, I would dance with any of those horrible *snobs* Rose is talking to?"

"One of those horrible English snobs is the rich Mr. Jones," says Roger, stroking his moustache, and remembering the lesson in matchmaking he received before dinner from Rose. "I thought Mr. Jones was an admirer of yours, Belinda?" he adds, looking inquiringly into the girl's upturned face.

"An admirer—I suppose Rose told you that? As if I went in for admirers—I! Do I look as if that kind of rubbish was in my line of life?"

Roger hesitates. His heart goes out towards this poor neglected child, with her tattered clothes and shaky morals, and sweet imploring women's eyes; but, with the best will in the world, he finds it difficult to be kind to her. Every look, every tone, every smallest gesture of Belinda O'Shea's so utterly sets patronage or compassion at defiance.

"And Mr. Jones cannot dance round dances," she goes on presently; "they send the blood to his 'ead. Captain Temple," her voice softening in a moment, a wistful pleading expression coming round her lips, "do round dances send the blood to your 'ead, I wonder?"

Roger had a flower in his button-hole, an oleander bud, abstracted for him by the fair fingers of his betrothed from one of the bouquets upon the dinner-table; and as she speaks, Belinda, with all a child's ignorance of shame, removes this flower from its place, raises it an instant to her face, then fastens it in the waistbelt of her own dress.

"Do round dances send the blood to your 'ead, Captain Temple? I *should* so like a waltz, if you will have one with me."

"If? Why, of course I will, my dear child! You should have asked me sooner. Hark! there is the waltz beginning now. We shall be just in time."

He forgets Rose and Rose's strong opinions as to fast dancing; forgets that Belinda is still in the disgraceful frock and ill-matched stockings; forgets everything but the child's wistful pleading face. One waltz, poor little girl? Ay, and as many more as she chooses, thinks kind-hearted Roger; and takes her hand and leads her bravely within under the gaslights and among the silks and satins, yes, close to the owner of the pink satin, and the fan, whose blue eyes glance at him no longer.

"I may as well take my hat off, though," cries Belinda, preparing to start, without loss of time, "Hi! Costa boy! Guard!"

She flings back her ragged hat to the old dog, who ever since Roger's appearance upon the scene has been watching matters suspiciously, and is now peering with jealous eyes round a corner of one of the doors. Then she puts her slim sunburnt hand upon Captain Temple's arm.

"... I asked you to dance just to try you," she whispers, when they have gone once or twice round the room. "I thought, yes, and I hoped, you would be too ashamed to be seen with me, and then I should have had a good excuse for hating you. But you were not. You are a better fellow at heart than I took you for, although you are——"

"Although I am—what, my dear?"

"I wish you would leave off calling me 'my dear,' and—and I can never talk when I am dancing," says Belinda, illogically.

"At all events you have not made up your mind to hate me yet?" whispers Roger in her ear.

Fate lands them, when the waltz is over, exactly opposite Rosie and her train of attendants, and Roger Temple, for the first time in his life, feels himself a coward! Something about the lips of the little pink-and-white woman who owns him makes him tremble—yes, tremble. Let men who are not lovers laugh in the flippant levity of their souls if they will.

"What a *way* Rose is in!" says Belinda, who possesses to the full the cruel acumen of her age. "I remember that particular smile of hers so well! It always came before my worst whippings."

Roger is silent. That his Rose possesses some few thorns he knows, innocuous feminine prickles of jealousy, vanity, and the like. How if little tempers be added to the list, the little tempers of an exacting woman of for—— But no; not even in imagination will Roger's chivalrous heart go within a hundred miles of that obnoxious numeral.

He shifts the subject and puts off the lecture that he knows to be in store for him by proposing that they shall go outside again. "Does Belinda mind the smell of a pipe? If not——"

"Mind?" the girl interrupts him. "Now just, once and for all, Captain Temple, understand this—Belinda minds nothing. What do you pay for tobacco in England? Sixteen shillings, twenty francs, a pound? Well, the next time I go to Irun, if I can only run the Custom House I shall bring you back some real Spanish in my pocket. Cheating the government? Oh, we don't trouble our heads about governments in this country; we smuggle whatever we can, and are thankful. You save one franc fifty on the pound of tobacco, and get a better weed, Sir, into the bargain."

They go outside, where Costa, bearing the hat between his teeth joins them; he lays it down at the feet of his little mistress, and with a low, half impatient, half loving bark, thrusts his nose beneath her hand for a caress.

"This is the best friend I have on earth, Captain Temple; he would pull you down—oh, as soon as look at you, if I held up my finger. Would you not, Costa?'

Costa, at this appeal, moves stealthily round to Roger Temple and criticises his heels, dog-fashion.

"Here, poor fellow—here, Costa!" says Roger, holding out his hand.

And, wonder of wonders to Belinda, Costa crouches, fawns, licks it! Evidently, whether she likes her father's successor or not (and she is doing her best, yes, did her best throughout every moment of the waltz, to detest him) Costa means to accept Roger Temple as a friend.

She calls the dog off instantly. "I did not think *you* would fawn on new-comers, Costa. Down with you—down! I want none of your hypocritical attentions. You are the first of my stepmamma's favourites I have ever known Costa speak to, Sir. You should see his delicious hatred of Burke and Mr. Jones."

"Ah, dogs understand some matters better than we understand them, Belinda. Costa has seen too much of life to put all men in the same category as you do."

They saunter forth into the night, side by side—this southern night, which is but a whiter, more voluptuous day; balmy as an English summer noon, the air so clearly lustrous that every remotest object on sea and land stands out, as though 'twere chiselled in silver, against the profound purple of the sky.

Roger Temple lights his pipe and begins (a little way Roger has in most feminine society) to feel his heart grow soft. Belinda whistles.

"Will you take my arm, my dear? I beg your pardon. I must try not to disobey orders again, but, you see, I cannot help forestalling events somewhat."

"Forestalling! What do you mean by forestalling?" says Belinda, turning on him sharply. "At what time, pray, of my life, or your life, or anybody's life, are Captain Temple and Belinda O'Shea going to be so wonderfully affectionate to each other—so wonderfully familiar?"

"Well, I should hope, when they live under the same roof together," answers Roger kindly. "Before very long, yes, before many more weeks are past, you must know that I look forward to your staying with us for good, Belinda. You have had quite enough, I think—I—I mean, Rosie thinks—of Miss Burke's protection. Surely you will allow me to speak to you as I should to my own little daughter then?"

"Your daughter? I am nobody's daughter!" she cries quickly. "I hate the sound of the word. I hate step-relationships. There was a time once—but now I have no one on the face of the earth I love; I want no one. And as to living with you and Rose, I prefer knocking about the world with Burke, by long odds, thank you. We are 'Miss Burke' and 'Miss O'Shea' always. We don't like each other, and we *don't pretend we don't*. We are not any kind of relations, or step-relations, heaven be thanked!"

The bitterness, the suppressed passion of her childish voice, do but soften Roger's heart towards her more and more. "Allow me to offer you my arm, Miss O'Shea, will you?"

"No, I thank you, Captain Temple; I find it quite hot enough walking alone. We are not used to such fine manners, are we, Costa, in our class of life?

> "'Pour toute la nature
> Quand boire a tant d'appas,
> Pourquoi la créature
> Ne boirait-elle pas?
> Buvons, chantons, et fêtons, tour à tour,
> Et l'ivresse, l'ivresse, l'ivresse et l'amour!'"

Belinda sings out these delightful optimist sentiments at the very top of her voice, then races away with Costa along the sandy slopes. When Roger catches her up, a hundred yards or so further on, all the gravity of her mood has melted into wildest spirits.

"It was good fun, that waltz we had down at the Casino, Roger—if you call me 'my dear,' why should I not call you 'Roger'—'step-papa Roger?' I enjoyed it all the more because I knew how my espargottes, and my stockings, and everything about me *riled* Rosie. But for real dancing— bah! if you want to see that you should come with me to the Place Ithurbida, and see how the peasant girls dance the bolera. It is not the third of a kilo away; I can hear the tambourines from this; and I'll promise to bring you back safe and sound, Roger; and—and Rosie is so happy with her young men."

She pleads to him, the soft night shining on her lips and eyes; and for the first time it occurs to Roger Temple that this wild little Arab child will be a pretty girl some day.

"Take me where you will, Belinda. I do not believe in you overmuch, but I believe in Costa. I am sure Costa would not stand quietly by and see me murdered."

"Ah, that shows how much you know of Costa. Did I not say you were a good judge of character? However, you need not be afraid. If I owed my enemy a grudge—mind, I only say 'if' " (but even as she qualifies her speech thus, malice indescribable lurks in her voice)—"if I owed my worst enemy a grudge, I would sooner let him live his fate out than put an end to his sufferings quickly. However, these are affairs of Spain, Roger, not of yours or mine . . . How sentimentally you gaze at everything!" He is gazing, if the truth be told, at her face. "You think this a most romantic spot where you are standing, no doubt?"

The spot *is* romantic, in its own rugged way, and seen by this starlight, which flatters old nature as a court portrait painter flatters women's faces. A broad Salvator-Rosa-looking sierra of arid turf, dotted here and there by a low white cross or stunted cypress, and with the dead unbroken blue of the Atlantic for background.

"You are standing over one great vault, Sir. St. Jean is healthy to a proverb, the Basque people say, except when we get the pestilence. Unfortunately, we get the pestilence pretty often, and then we have to be buried, not by ones and twos, but dozens, just wherever our friends can find room to dig trenches. I shall bring Rose and Mr. Jones up here some fine evening, make them sit down on one of these dear little mounds, and go into dear little raptures about the beauties of the climate and the scenery, and then inform them that they are sitting on dead men's bones. Bones—whole skeletons by scores! Only yesterday I saw the children playing *fossette*, I don't know how you say it in English, into a skull."

"And so naturally the place is a favourite haunt of yours?" remarks Roger. "Just the kind of taste I should have expected from a person of your grave and melancholy character."

"I would sooner keep company with skulls than fools, any day," retorts the girl, with a shrug of the shoulders. "Perhaps in years to come, when you have had as much experience of—of different varieties of intellect as I have had, you will come to the same opinion."

She leads the way down a rough bullock track or gully that diverges at this point from the shore, and a few minutes' walking brings them out upon the main road, ere railroads were, the world's highway to Spain, but seldom traversed now save by outlying bands of Carlists, or by the baggage-mules and ox-drays of the country people. Straight before them are the mountains—transparent wondrous violet in the shadows, faint alabaster (for the moon will be here anon) along the crests. The river, the lights of the town, gleam beneath. From the Place Ithurbida, a thicket of olives and cork trees close at hand, rise sounds of music—barbaric blood-stirring dance music, about as much like the thread-bare Parisian "tinkle-tinkle" of the casino waltzes, as the smell of the moorlands in September is like a barber's shop.

"Now you shall see dancing in earnest," says Belinda, arching her slender arms cachuca-fashion above her head, and her whole lithe figure seeming to become instinct on the moment with life and music. "Tra, la-la, la-la, lira, la lira, la lira!"

The orchestra is composed of a Basque tambourine and bagpipes, both instruments played by one old woman in rags, with castanet accompaniment *ad libitum* from the fingers of the performers. The corps de ballet consists of three couples of men and girls, all of the lowest order of the people ; not a shoe or stocking between them, but artists every one, if originality and fire, joined to the most perfect power of expression, the most finished neatness in execution, may be said to constitute art. These Basques dance as they smuggle, drink, gamble—with passion. Money-seeking as the French, pleasure-loving as the Spaniards, every hour of these people's vivid lives they *live*. Imagine Northern peasants, for pleasure, after a summer day's toil, dancing cachucas and fandangos till midnight!

Belinda, at Roger's side remains a silent spectator throughout one dance; with the first notes of the next her feet begin to twinkle.

"This is the Basque bolero, the national dance," she whispers to him; "but there are none of the best dancers here to-night. You should see the Gitanas who come down from the hill-country at fair-time, or "—little witch! as if the thought had suddenly struck her—as if it were not expressly for this that she had lured him hither,—" or you should see me. Will you see me dance a bolero, Captain Temple?"

"Some time or another, my dear child; some evening at Rosie's hotel, when——"

"Now, this moment! out of doors, to real Basque music, or never! What! do you think I would dance a bolero *on a floor*, with Rose shaking her head, and describing how nicely the young ladies used to turn their toes out at Miss Ingram's? I dance for you, Sir, now or never. If you are shocked, you know, you can easily walk off in another direction, and pretend you don't belong to me."

Her slight little form flits away into an open space between the trees, six or eight yards distant from the principal performers; and there, partnerless, unashamed as was ever court duchess during the stately performance of a minuet, the Earl of Liskeard's grand-daughter dances her bolero. All the originality of gesture, the supple strength, the staying power of the peasants, Belinda possesses to the full; but she possesses something more, poor child!—the graces born of mind as well as matter, the delicate, exquisite alternations of fire and languor, which are the very poetry of true dancing, and of whose seductive charm she is only too profoundly ignorant.

Roger watches her with pleasure as regards the gratification of his artistic sense, and at the same time with curiously poignant pain. He has lived too long in India not to be reminded of Nautch girls and their performances by this kind of exhibition; and Rosie's animadversions on the subject of Belinda return with unpleasant clearness to his mind. The peasants, with the perfect natural breeding that characterises their race, take no further notice of the child than by a smile or a nod as they pass her in the evolutions of the dance. When it is over they seat themselves on the turf, the girls together, the men a little apart, and all begin chatting in that liquid bastard Sanscrit of theirs which of itself is music. Belinda trips gaily back to Roger's side.

"I dance tolerably well? I dance better than any of those fine die-away Hermiones and Dolores at the casino, don't I?" she exclaims, holding up her eager face within about a foot of Roger's in the moonlight.

The bolero has lent new animation to Belinda's expressive features; her deep Irish eyes are all aglow, her parted lips tremble. Roger Temple discovers that there are materials not only for a pretty, but for a very pretty girl, in his future stepdaughter, and can by no means bring himself up to the sternly virtuous spirit of admonition which would befit the occasion.

"You dance a vast deal too well, Belinda—too well for the present company, I mean."

"Ah! those are your English prejudices—Mrs. Grundy, Sir. I heard the same story from poor Mr. Jones this morning. My 'company' as you call it, is every bit as good as that mob of Madrid shopkeepers we danced among at the casino. Don't you know that the Basques are a people of nobles? Why, the very beggars wear their rags with an air that makes you feel the vulgarity of soap-and-water; and as to the bullock-drivers, there is not one of them but has a pedigree . . . so long! and who feels—yes, and looks noble, every inch of him."

"Then let the Basque nobles dance boleros by themselves," says Roger. "I am of a jealous disposition, child;

it does not please me that your pretty dances and your pretty self should be at the mercy of every stranger who may happen to pass along a public roadway."

Up leaps the blood into her brown cheeks. The reproof, if reproof it be, savours of a tenderness to which she has been so long unused, a tenderness that sinks with such dangerous sweetness on her heart.

"Do I dance prettily?" Her eyes for the first time fall beneath his; she trifles, a little abashed, with the pomegranate bud in her waistbelt. "I made you come here because—oh, because I wanted to shock you as I shock Mr Jones and Rose. But do I really dance prettily—better than the peasant girls?"

"So much better, Belinda, that I should like to bid you never dance another bolero or cachuca while you live."

She stands a moment irresolute, then turns from him without a word. Vanity, childish triumph, and a burning, perfectly new sense of womanly shame, are holding the oddest conflict imaginable in Belinda's heart, and keeps her dumb.

"If I had only the right to exact a promise of you," goes on Roger, possessing himself, as he speaks, of her hand, and pressing it with kindly warmth.

"But you have not the right—no, not as much as Augustus Jones has!" she exclaims, snatching her hand away abruptly, and bursting into a peal of laughter. "Augustus *might* have bought me, perhaps, with a franc's worth of macaroons, but you—you! Reserve your jealousy, Captain Temple, for the time when Rose takes to dancing boleros with the peasants! And as for me—

"'Buvons, chantons, et fêtons, tour à tour,
 Et l'ivresse, l'ivresse, l'ivresse et l'amour.'"

She sings the bacchanalian chorus with greater spirit than ever; then pirouetting the step of the bolero as she goes, disappears among the olives, nor joins Captain Temple again until he is within a dozen paces of the casino.

Mrs. O'Shea, star-gazing on the terrace with Augustus, receives them with honeyed smiles. Admiration acts upon Rosie's moral faculties like wine; and she has really been a good deal admired this evening—or a good deal stared at, which comes very much to the same thing. When one reaches a certain age it is not wisest to accept "attention" just as one receives it, without criticising its quality too closely.

"Oh, you naughty, naughty children!" She nestles her hand at once under Roger's arm, nor takes it away again. "We have been looking for you everywhere. What a *nice* waltz you had! I was *so* glad to see Captain Temple dancing with you, Belinda! But I am afraid you found those sandal things *dreadfully* inconvenient to dance in, dear!"

The italics, the plentiful notes of admiration, convey venom, trebly distilled, to Belinda's sensitive ear. Roger hears only the soft veiled voice, feels only the plump pressure of his beloved one's hand upon his arm; and he "blesses her unaware." Dear, gentle, timid Rose! How sweet these womanly women are, even if a trifle silly! The pungent piquancy of a semi-barbarian like Belinda, may be tasteful, as sherry and bitters are tasteful, on occasion. But for honest every-day consumption, morning, noon, and night, what can be compared to the wholesomeness of table beer—table beer, with only just the least little suspicion of a tendency to turn sour!

"This is really not half a bad sort of view," says Augustus, pulling at his wristbands with the self-consciousness of a man who wants to be unconcerned, and addressing the Atlantic. "On the right we have the ruins of St. Barbe, still bearing marks of the English guns of thirteen, on the left the coast of Spain, while close at hand——"

"Rises the gloomy church tower of St. Jean de Luz," cries Belinda, imitating the poor wretch's pedantic company-voice to admiration; "that sacred edifice in which Louis the Fourteenth was formally betrothed to Maria Theresa, Infanta of Spain, in the year of our Lord sixteen hundred and sixty. How long will it be, Mr. Jones, before your great book of travels is published? 'Twould be a pity, upon my word, that so much valuable research should be wasted!"

"Belinda—Belinda, my dear, how can you!" says Rose, admonishingly. "Mr. Jones, why do you let her? I am sure it is all most interesting. Poor dear Louis the Fourteenth and Marie Antoinette—we read the Peninsular War straight through at Miss Ingram's. But Belinda is such a quiz. Really it seems like something in a novel, doesn't it, Roger, to be so near Spain?"

This is, literally, Rose's conversational style reduced to orthography; style that one may call the absolute perfected vacuity of human speech; but yet that, lisped by a pretty woman, now making play with her eyes, now suffering giggling eclipses behind her pocket-handkerchief, now pressing her fingers confidentially on your arm, is not without its charm to the superior intellect of man.

Roger replies, "Yes, indeed, Rosie!" a safe, unmeaning answer, that he keeps always ready for the foolish little babble of his betrothed.

Augustus, who, like other unhappy young men of his class, regards silence as a lapse of breeding, once more starts a subject.

"How many persons would Captain Temple suppose now, this casino might be capable of holding?" He suspects that Roger dislikes him; he knows that he detests Roger; and shifts from one leg to another, and fidgets at his glove-button (Augustus Jones wears yellow gloves at these casino balls) as he addresses him.

"How many people? Really Mr. Jones, I have not the

smallest notion." Capital fellow though Roger be, to those who know him and whom he likes, I feel that when he addresses men like Mr. Jones I cannot altogether clear him from the imputation of "shutting his eyes as he talks." "Kind of thing I never guessed in my life. Belinda, can you tell Mr. Jones how many people the St. Jean de Luz casino holds?"

"Of course, I cannot," answers Belinda, with her crushing brusquerie. "Who in their senses would ask such a question, unless they were collecting materials for a guide-book? Now if you wanted to know about the people themselves, I might enlighten you."

"Enlighten us by all means," says Roger Temple. And he moves, despite a slight unwillingness in Rosie's fingers, nearer to the girl's side. "Begin with the little lady in pink satin. There she is, opposite, looking over her fan at the gentleman with the ferocious moustache. Do you know anything about her?"

"Anything? I should just say I did! And about the man with the moustache, too! Why, those are the people from Burgos, who . . ."

And then, such a story as Rosie, straightlaced, over-scrupulous Rosie, is forced to listen to! Such a story, succeeded by such a dozen others! Constantly frequenting the society of gamins younger than herself, Belinda has picked up all the watering-place wickedness afloat, simply as a gamin picks up wickedness, and details it without a blush.

And she tells her stories well; dramatizing a scene in Spanish here, throwing in some caustic bit of mimicry there, keeping her characters vivid and living, before her audience, always.

"We have had enough, more than enough, scandal," cries Rose, at last. "You have quite taken my breath away Belinda. These may be the moralities of foreign watering-places, the subjects of foreign conversation, but they are not *English!* I declare, when we were girls, we did not know the meaning of evil!"

"How hard of comprehension you must have been, my dear," observes Belinda cheerfully. "I suppose that was in the innocent days when you first met Captain Temple?"

The taunt makes Roger himself wince. The innocent days—when he first whispered his passion to old Shelmadeane's young wife beside the hippopotamus!

"You are severe this evening, Belinda," he remarks coldly. "You make no distinction between friend and foe. Rose, my dear," bending over the widow and whispering—yet not so low but that Belinda's ear can catch every lover-like syllable, "is it not late for you to be out, after all the fatigues of your journey? Let me take you back to the hotel, dearest. You look pale."

"Oh, but, Belinda!" says Rose generously, and making a feint of quitting her lover's arm. "Don't, anybody, think of me. See Belinda home first."

"Thanks very much, Rose," cries the girl. "As Belinda has been seeing myself home (only she never had a home) during the last four years, she will probably be quite capable of doing the same to-night."

"If—if I may be allowed?" And Mr. Jones puts himself forward, in obedience to a glance he receives from Rose. "It is too late for Miss O'Shea to pass through the town without an escort."

"Miss, O'Shea has got Costa for her escort," begins Belinda, with her usual sturdy independence; then, abruptly, she discovers that Roger Temple is watching her face, and a new freak of perversity takes possession of her. "Miss O'Shea has got Costa, but she will be only too glad of *your* protection, now and at all times, Mr. Jones!" smiling affectionately at Jones with her lips, and mocking him, ridiculing him, despising him with her eyes.

". . . You will see if that is not a match," remarks Rose, as the two figures walk away together in the moonlight. "I was so much obliged to you, my dear, for taking her off my hands this evening; it gave me such a nice long talk with Mr. Jones, and I am convinced he is *serious*. What is more, Roger, in spite of all her flighty manner, I am convinced that Belinda will accept him; indeed, my only fear is that he will be shocked by her over-readiness. A young girl telling an eligible man that she would be glad ' now and at all times' for his protection!"

"Recollect her age, Rose. You must not take, au pied de la lettre, every word that a madcap child like Belinda chooses to utter."

"I take people's speeches, and their actions, too, as I find them," answers Rose, ignoring the quotation. Rosa ignores everything in the universe that she does not herself understand. "And I do not forget that Belinda is of Vansittart blood. Like mother like daughter." Proud though she be of the connection, Cornelius O'Shea's widow can never refrain from flinging her little pebble at poor dead Lady Elizabeth's memory. "We all know what kind of reputation the Vansittart women have."

"The reputation of more than common beauty, I have been told," remarks Roger, with an air of innocence.

"She has taken his arm—actually! When we were girls, such a thing was never thought of, until one was formally engaged. Belinda has taken Mr. Jones's arm—do you see?"

"Yes, I see, I see," answers Roger Temple, not without impatience. Curious anomaly, if anything pertaining to the relations of men and women can ever be called anomalous, Rosie's lover is sensible of a distinct pang of jealousy at this moment. "Any girl of seventeen would encourage any fellow who had carriages and diamonds to offer her—as you ought to know, Rose."

"Belinda, most of all," acquiesces the widow, with one of her prettiest sighs. "It has gone out of fashion for young girls to sacrifice interest to the Affections, as we used."

Roger thinks of Mr. Shelmadeane, and is silent.

CHAPTER VII.

MAMMON WINS HIS WAY.

WHITE with moonlight, astir with the life and joyousness of the southern night, are the narrow streets of St. Jean de Luz, as Mr. Jones and his companion proceed towards what may by courtesy be called Belinda's home. Ladies, with fan and mantilla, returning bareheaded from the casino ball; itinerant serenaders twanging guitars for money—alas! is there to be no poetry left in life?—beneath the projecting iron balconies; stately hidalgos in cloaks; statelier beggars in tatters; every here and there a *patio*, or garden, odorous with citron-flowers, pomegranate, myrtle; and for back-ground the mountains, just one shade deeper iris than the arch of tremulous heaven overhead.

Could hour or scene be more auspicious for a lover? Could hour or scene better dispose a girl's imagination towards a declaration of love?

They walk for a considerable time in silence, Belinda and Mr. Jones. At last, "I hope you have forgiven me for not feeding Costa on macaroons?" whispers the young man, pressing her unresponsive hand ever so little to his side.

"Do you, Mr. Jones?—why?" She accepted his arm out of sheerest perversity, and because she guessed that certain eyes were watching her; but her heart feels wicked against poor Augustus, wicked against the whole bright world which forms a background for Roger Temple and for Rose. "When *I* know people detest me, I would much rather be without their forgiveness than with it."

Not an encouraging answer for a man on the eve of proposing. But Mrs. O'Shea's wary arts during that starlit conversation on the terrace have brought up Mr. Jones's resolution to the sticking point. So much familiar talk of Lady Althea and Lord Lionel—"Belinda's nearest relations, Mr. Jones, the people, whenever our dear Belinda does settle in London, with whom she and her husband must be constantly *and intimately thrown.*" So much familiar talk, I say, about possible cousins in the peerage, not unmingled with suggestions that, in our dear Belinda's position, a happy early union, rather than large settlements, is what Rose's step-maternal heart yearns after, have made Mr. Jones resolute to win or give up all to-night.

He does not love, he sees no remotest chance of bringing himself to love, this meagre, dark-skinned, bitter-tongued mite of an earl's granddaughter. But Jones is not a man to be turned aside from any project, commercial or matrimonial, by obstacle so paltry as personal likes or dislikes. The earliest sacred truth instilled into his childish soul, his highest mature conception of moral law, is—that Christians and Englishmen should buy in the cheapest market whatever article they require. He, Jones, requires the article Birth; has hunted it up and down many English watering-places, as men of the Cornelius O'Shea genus hunt money, and now has it under his hand, to be bought for a song—(did not Rosie wisely throw in the hint about modest settlements?) the only difficulty being as to the article's consent. But after sunning himself in the widow's smiles, and listening to the widow's silky flatteries during the past hour and a half, Mr. Jones cannot but feel that he is a very captivating fellow, indeed, in women's eyes, and entertains but little fear as to that.

"I have never been fortunate enough to find you at home yet, Miss O'Shea." He makes this next attempt at tender talk just as they reach the Maison Lohobiague, on the third floor of which Miss Burke and Belinda lodge. "I should like," sentimentally, "to see the apartment where you spend your time—if I might?"

It seems to him that the task of bringing her to terms will be easier of accomplishment indoors than out. Never yet has he seen Belinda within four walls, and the idea strikes him that she may prove more manageable within a restricted space: like a squirrel in a cage, a colt within a pound, or any other inferior animal whom it is man's supreme pleasure to tame and subjugate.

"The apartment where I spend my time—Burke's den? Well, if you want to see it, you had better use your legs and walk up now. Miss Burke, as you know, is away; our servant—actually we have a servant, Mr. Jones, just to set our soup going of a morning—went off to the bull-fight at Fontarabia yesterday, and has not appeared since. So you must not expect to see things in apple-pie order."

She quits his arm, bestows a series of hugs and farewells on Costa—the poor old dog, well-trained, stopping discreetly three or four paces away from Miss Burke's threshold, then vanishes out of sight beneath an overhanging stone porte-cochère, or archway; whither Mr. Jones, his dapper feet tortured by the stones, his yellow-kidded hands extended to save his nose from collision with the wall, follows her.

The Maison Lohobiague is one of those towering fifteenth-century Basque palaces, of which three or four still stand, fast-crumbling, alas! into dust, beside the harbour of St. Jean de Luz. The Infanta of Spain lodged in the Lohobiague, says oral history, on the occasion of her betrothal to Louis the Fourteenth. Now 'tis tenanted out in sets of furnished lodgings, low rented, on account of rats, dry-rot, mould, and other such draw-backs to mediæval romance, but deliciously cool in summer by reason of the narrow semi-Moorish windows, thick walls, and vaulted balconies; and with the noblest panorama of river, fertile plain, and distant lonely mountain sierra for outlook.

The dark, winding staircase seems trebly dark after the intense moonlight of the streets; and Mr. Jones, a careful man, not only as regards moral, but bodily risks, pauses at the bottom.

"Come along, if you are coming," rings out Belinda's voice from airy heights overhead. "There is plenty of light when once you get up here, only look after your shins meanwhile."

The "plenty of light" proceeds from a solitary oil-lamp, which sheds its dim religious rays before the figure of a saint on the landing of the second floor. A grotesquely-tawdry female saint, of Basque or Spanish origin, life-sized, ghastly-hued; with a laced-pocket-handkerchief, with blood streaming from her martyred brow and hands, a necklace of huge mock brilliants on her throat, a pair of satin slippers that may have been white once, say at the betrothal of Louis the Fourteenth, upon her feet.

"We live one story higher still," says Belinda, Mr. Jones stopping to turn up his British nose at this work of sacerdotal art; "and unless Juanita happens to have left a candle, I shall have to entertain you in the dark. However, there is the moon."

"And—and the brightness of your eyes, Belinda," says Jones, groping his way up the steep staircase after her.

"And what?" shouts the girl, sharply, through the darkness. "There is such an echo, Mr. Jones—no hearing a word unless you speak more distinctly. What did you say would light us?"

But something, either in the tone of her voice or in the

distance which separates them, restrains Mr. Jones from again launching into the hazardous region of compliment.

Under the lawful régime of Miss Burke the outer door of the apartment is always kept virtuously locked after dark; but this, like other precautionary rules of life, is set at nought when Belinda, as at present, holds the rudder of government. Half ajar stands a huge oaken door, blackened with time, crusted with dirt : a door as old, probably, as the solid masonry of the house. On a vigorous push from the girl's hand it creaks slowly back upon its hinges, and Mr. Jones is introduced to " Burke's den," a room bigger than an Isle of Wight church, the roof joisted and innocent of all modern refinement of lath and plaster, the walls of the indescribable smoky grey of ages. Vast cobwebbed pictures of saints in different stages of burning or mutilation—French studies, probably, after Ribera, exaggerations, nightmares, of that master's most repulsive realism—hang around. Saints and cobwebs may indeed be said to furnish the room. Of furniture proper there are—a table that was once carved and gilt, now in the last stage of rickety decay, and of which one leg is propped up by a pile of battered books ; a lofty pier-glass, over-dim with antiquity for purposes of reflection ; three crippled chairs, piled pell-mell at the present moment in a corner ; and a shelf, containing in all about twelve pieces of crockery of different sizes and patterns. " I am an Ishmaelite by choice," Miss Burke will say, with the conscious proud humility of intellect, to such straggling acquaintance as chance ever gives her to entertain. " The frivolous details of upholstery do not concern me. Climate, nature, association with the mighty minds of the past—*these* to me are the necessities of life ! "

Mr. Jones looks round him open-mouthed, Belinda having been fortunate enough to find a candle, whose solitary light barely pierces from end to end of the sombre shadowy room.

"And you—you live here?" he exclaims with unaffected amazement. "What a place—what pictures! It gives one the horrors to look at them." Only Mr. Jones is thinking a little nervously over what he is going to say next, and calls it "'orrors."

"Well, yes—the Maison Lohobiague is not furnished according to Clapham taste," retorts Belinda, with her frank impertinence. "But it suits me better. I like the old shabby room, Mr. Jones, and the 'orrid pictures, and the cobwebs; yes, and I should be very sorry to exchange them for any stuccoed Cockney gentility. I have lived here two years, off and on; Miss Burke has made it a sort of headquarters in all her comings and goings, and I have grown to the place. If Burke would only get killed on a railway, or made professoress, or anything, I should be quite content to stop in the Lohobiague with Costa, always."

And now, Augustus feels is the time to crash down on this poor pauper child with the magnificence of his offer. "Miss O'Shea—Belinda," he cries, coming up beside her very close, "there is no necessity for you to spend your days in these miserable foreign places any longer. Since I saw you this afternoon I—ahem—I have been talking to your mamma."

"Step-mamma. If you are not accurate you are nothing."

"And I have made my mind up—I have made my mind up fully," says Jones, with magnanimity, "as to my line of conduct. There may seem, there *are* disparities"—he glances, with an air of condescension at the girl's dress, at the appointments of the meagre room; "still, as Mrs. O'Shea says, six months of the first educational advantages in England would work wonders, and, at our age, we can afford to wait, can we not?"

"I could answer better if I had a glimmering notion of what you mean by 'we.' Are you going to school again, Mr. Jones? Mind your H's, you know, if you do."

"Belinda!" his voice shakes, his colour rises. ("How hideous he is!" communes Belinda within herself. "How the mosquito bites glow and radiate from out that purple blush!") "Do you think you ever—I mean—I know—I never" . . . confound it all, why will the girl fix those hard eyes of her's upon his face? . . . " never saw any one so likely to make me happy. Oh, come, you mustn't take your hand away!" which she does, with unmistakable energy, the moment she feels his touch. "I will not let you go till you answer me. Belinda, could you ever care for me enough to be my wife?"

He has stumbled through it as well, perhaps, as the majority of men stumble through the most momentous question of their lives. Belinda, who has never before heard a declaration, or read of a declaration, or imagined a declaration, thinks the exhibition pitiable, and tells him so.

"You are a more complete fool than I took you for, Mr. Jones. If you really want me—*me*—to marry you, why not say so like a rational being, instead of stammering and hesitating and blushing, like a schoolboy ashamed to speak the truth?"

Mr. Jones stands, silently recovering his nerve after the plunge.

"It will, I know, meet the wishes of Mrs. O'Shea and of Captain Temple," he remarks at last, almost humbly.

"What will?"

"Our marriage, Belinda."

"Did they tell you so?"

"Mrs. O'Shea lead me to believe—"

"Rose leads everybody to believe everything. And he— Captain Temple?"

"It can be no interest of Captain Temple's to put himself in the way of your settlement, I should say."

She turns from him; she walks quickly to the further end of the room; a certain dignity, child though she be, in every movement of her poor little ragged figure. Then she comes back to the young man's side and looks steadily, with her honest eyes, into his.

"A thing like this can't be decided in a moment, Mr. Jones. If you want, really and truly, to marry me, you must, I suppose, have some good reasons for doing so. That is not my business, however. Every one is free to have his own crotchets about happiness. But what I do want to know, and what I dare say you can tell me, is—why should I marry you?"

"I should hope, a little, because you like me," suggests Augustus, trying with imperfect success to throw a lover-like warmth into his voice. "That is the reason generally, I believe, for which young ladies accept men."

"Is it, indeed? I thought liking had nothing whatever to do with such things. I thought the lover said, 'I can offer such a house, carriage, servants, diamonds, on condition that you take me for a husband.' And then that the young lady reckoned up the sweets and the sours together, and answered 'Yes' or 'No,' according to whether she found the bargain good."

"Is that the kind of way you wish me to address you, Miss O'Shea?"

"It is the best way for you to address me if you want to get a sensible answer, Mr. Jones."

She perches herself on a corner of the rickety table, tilts her hat on the back of her head, and swinging her sandalled feet to and fro in the air, begins—as coolly as though she were scoring up the points at paume—to reckon the items of the projected "bargain."

"Carriage, so much; diamonds, so much; house, so much. We will begin with the house. How large a house, exactly, should you and I have to live in at Clapham?"

"I am not joking, and you are," replies Jones sullenly. "Of course, if you do not choose to take the thing seriously, I have nothing more to say."

"Well, would you mind my having my supper first? I am as hungry as a wolf, Sir. Burke leaves me on a kind of board wages when she goes off literaturing, and I have not eaten a mouthful since your macaroons. You will not mind? Thanks. And while I eat, you know, you can make yourself agreeable, tell me all the delightful projects you and Rosie have been laying out for my future welfare."

Belinda's supper consists of a big slice of household bread, and another rather bigger one of melon, washed down by cold water. Having produced these refreshments from the shelf, which at once answers as dresser, larder, and pantry, she resumes her former place on the corner of the table, and unincumbered by knife, fork, or plate sups.

Mr. Jones, who, like other unwholesome-blooded, city-bred persons, distrusts all wholesome, natural simple food, watches her with a kind of pitying horror. Melon at night! cold water! brown bread, devoured in half-pound slices!

"Yes, my living does not cost much," cries Belinda, interpreting his looks correctly. "That will be one blessing, at least, for my husband. And if he liked to pitch his tent farther south it would cost less. Talk of a Clapham villa! Why, you need not have a house at all, for more than three months in the year, down at Granada, there are such jolly arches and walls to sleep under; and the wine of the country, fine strong wine, that gets into your head directly, is as cheap as water, and you can buy a day's fruit for five gramos. I should say," meditatively, "a married pair, of quiet habits and unambitious minds, could live handsomely in Granada on twenty-five francs a week; yes, and be able to treat themselves to a theatre or a bull-fight of a Sunday as well."

"Twenty-five francs a week!—fifty pounds a year!" says Augustus. "Not the quarter of what I should allow *my* wife for pin-money."

A sharply-contrasted picture they make at this moment, reader, these two people who are discussing the propriety of spending their lives together: Belinda, with her mischievous Murillo eyes and gleaming teeth, devouring melon, and swinging her ragged feet to and fro as she philosophises on the nothingness of wealth; Mr. Jones, yellow-gloved, London-coated, and with his smug, calculating Leadenhall Street face, watching her.

He is cleverish, worldly cleverish at least—the sons of most very successful men are that; but he has not a chance against the gamin astuteness, the keen mother wit of Belinda O'Shea. Devouring her bread and melon, rattling on with wild panegyrics of the delights of beggary, she sets herself to find out from him the precise extent of Rose's little intrigue on her behalf, the precise goodness of the "bargain" offered to her acceptance, and succeeds, aye, even as regards details. Such a carriage, such liveries, a couple of riding-horses, an opera-box, such a set of diamonds, as her wedding gift. Rose, to the utmost of her power, has sold her, and sold her advantageously; Captain Temple—well, Captain Temple a not unwilling witness to the transaction.

Now for her reply.

"I cannot imagine what put it into your head to think of me, Mr. Jones. Oh, I know why you came to St. Jean de Luz, of course; Rosie planned your tour for you! But what first put it into your head to think of me in that sort of light?" For a moment her long eyelashes shade her cheek, the cheek that neither pales nor reddens under his gaze. "I have not made myself over and above civil to you, have I?"

"Well no, not anything very particular," Mr. Jones assents.

"And I am sure I am not what you, with your fastidious tastes, would think ladylike"—oh the curl, imperceptible, perhaps, to Augustus, of her upper lip!—"nor what any one" with a thoroughly sincere sigh, this, "would think pretty. Now what, in the name of heaven, can make you wish to marry me?"

"I—I—because I love you," begins Jones, stammering.

"Tell that blague to some one else," interrupts the girl, with sudden passion, "not to me! If you loved me I should feel it—*here*," clasping her expressive brown hands to her breast, "just as I feel that Costa loves me, and I would marry you—yes, even you—to-morrow, out of gratitude, and if you had only a hundred a year instead of all the thousands you talk of. But you do not. You care no more for me than I for you, and so—"

"And so I suppose you will not marry me?" says Jones, with mortification, that he would fain hide under an air of banter.

Belinda hesitates, looks away from him. She is a child, with all a child's instinctive craving for the sweets of liberty, but she is a Bohemian as well, with all a Bohemian's keen appreciation of money, and of what money will bring. It would—it would be sweet, she feels, to wear finer dresses, richer jewels than Rosie's, to invite Rosie and Captain Temple condescendingly to dinner, lend them one's opera-box, take them for a drive occasionally in one's carriage. And then to bid good-bye for ever to Miss Burke! The thought of Augustus Jones as a life companion may be hideous, but half its hideousness vanishes, surely, if one remembers this—he would replace Miss Burke.

"I am certain I shall make you wretched, Mr. Jones, but as you seem, you and Rosie, to have set your minds on this engagement . . . stop, though! I must ask one thing. First, is your name on the door-plate—I mean of the Clapham villa? That I could not stand."

"My name *on a door-plate?*" says Jones, as indignantly as though the blood of the Howards ran in his veins. "Why, what do you take me for? No one but professional men, apothecaries, or that sort of thing, ever ticket their names outside on a door-plate."

"Well, then—I could never suit you nor you me, the whole thing is preposterous!—still, if you would like to try it, just as an experiment—"

He rushes forward rapturously.

"Oh, I thank you—very much obliged, indeed!" Belinda springs upon her feet, and puts herself in a not altogether unscientific attitude of self-defence. "We may be engaged, if you like, but I will have no fooleries of that kind. Do you hear me—I will not! Mr. Jones, you shall never kiss me."

And then, quick as thought itself, flashes on her the remembrance of the moment when her eyes first met Roger's this afternoon, of the hour spent with Roger alone under the stars, of the moment when he praised her—ah, with praise how unlike the fulsome compliments of this legitimate lover! and when vanity, shame, a minglement of feelings such as her life had never known before, held her dumb.

"Never kiss you! Not even when we are married, I suppose?" remarks Mr. Jones, unwisely jocular.

"Married—who talks of being married?" cries Belinda; such mutiny against her own weakness, such disdain, such mockery of her captor in her eyes!

"You talked a moment ago about trying the experiment, did you not?"

"I said that we might try being lovers—no, not lovers either—that we might try being engaged; and I keep to it. You are going away to visit the Pas de Roland, you know, to-morrow."

"Not now. I shall have no spare time for sight-seeing now," interrupts Augustus amatively.

"Why not? Because Rose is here? Oh, Rose has quite enough on her hands without you. You will go to the mountains to-morrow, and you will stay away four days, as you intended, and admire every waterfall, and rock, and ruin, Murray bids you. By that time I shall be used to the thought of—of Clapham, perhaps. Miss Burke will be back, for one thing, and I shall have had a good deal," with a sigh, this, "of Rose. I shall feel better disposed towards any change. Mr. Jones, if you will promise never, as long as you live, to kiss me, I dare say I shall not be very sorry to see you come back."

And not one other warmer word or promise can Augustus wring from her. She will try being engaged, minus lovemaking, as an experiment; and if he will promise never, as long as he lives, to kiss her, perhaps, after four days' absence, she may not be very sorry to see him return.

So much for his present chance of an alliance with the noble family of Vansittart.

As Mr. Jones walks back to the Hotel Isabella in the moonlight, he does not feel sure that he will have bought the article Birth quite so cheaply after all.

CHAPTER VIII.

VANITY v. CONSCIENCE.

MRS. AUGUSTUS JONES, Belinda Jones, Mr. and Mrs. Jones, Clapham.

So Belinda, when she is alone, rings every possible change upon her future titles as a matron, and finds each tuneless. But then the diamonds—reflection that, ere this, has governed the conduct of so many a wiser, older, better woman. Belinda's life, of late years, has not brought her into personal contact with many of the outward belongings of wealth. One tremendously showy and massive brilliant was wont to sparkle in Major O'Shea's neck-tie; but that, likelier than not, thinks the girl, with a sigh, was paste. Papa used to say, when he was in a moralising mood, that everything was paste in this degenerate nineteenth century. "There has been a bronze age, my child, and an iron age," Cornelius would tell her. "This is the age of paste. And, in the long run, the counterfeit answers just as well as the reality." If paste diamonds, in the long run, would answer as well as real ones, why become the wife of Mr. Jones, and live at Clapham for the sake of them? Ah, but there are the riding-horses as well—the riding-horses, the silk dresses, the opera-box.

Wistfully gazing through the open window at the sky,

Belinda thinks of the remote Belgravian days when her papa was in the first delightful flush of Rose's money. The days of dinner parties and balls, when even she, Belinda, wore pretty frocks, and occasionally tasted the society of lovely bare-necked beings, with flowers in her hair, silken trains, fans, lovers ; instead of watching them, forlornly from without, as she did to-night. How would *she* look bare-necked, with flowers in her hair, with a train, a fan, lovers? How if she should attempt a rehearsal of the effect (lovers excepted) with such rough materials as she may have at hand?

Miss Burke, as it chances, has left the key of her travelling-case in the lock. Alas, the frame of mind for wrong-doing given, and when does the demon, opportunity, fail any of us? And in Miss Burke's travelling-case lies, neatly folded, that lady's best black silk dress. In shorter time than it has taken me to write, Belinda, candle in hand, glides into the adjoining room, the sanctuary of Miss Burke's maiden charms, opens the case, gazes, vacillates—handles.

The skirt is too long, for Miss Burke is of loftier stature than herself, so much the grander will be her train. And the sleeves must be tucked up, and the bodice pinned down, and white lace, also of Miss Burke's, added, here and there, for lightness. Never in her life before has Belinda touched thread and needle, save under stress of direst necessity. But with the very first awakening of love in a young girl's heart awaken the instincts of millinery. She collects together such dislocated sewing implements as the household can boast ; with absorbed interest stitches down a fold here, puckers up a plait there ; finally skips lightly out of her own dingy Cinderella frock, and a minute later stands radiant, in the majesty of rustling silk, short sleeves, bare throat, and train—a young lady.

She is not an ugly girl, after all. So much the tarnished

glass upon Miss Burke's dressing-table assures her promptly. Her neck and shoulders look lily fair compared to the sun-tan of her face; her arms are delicately fashioned, and tolerably plump for seventeen. But the pig-tails! She snatches off the hideous frayed-out green ribbon, unplaits them, and behold—the ill-kempt neglected hair falls round her slender figure in waves of silky chestnut! A pair of gloves of Miss Burke's supplies an impromptu cushion, over which she coifs it high above her forehead, as the little Spanish blonde in pink (the blonde Roger Temple admired) was coiffed to-night. A scarlet passion-flower, wet with dew, from the balcony, finishes the picture.

Not ugly? Why she is pretty already—a year or two hence will be admirably so, prettier than was ever Rosie in her prime, thinks Belinda, gazing at her own transfigured self in a kind of rapture. The only thing she lacks now is jewellery—earrings, bracelets, a necklace for her throat; the Jones diamonds, in short. Pending the possession of these could no substitute be found to give one some imperfect foreshadowing of their splendour?

To the female conscience, once fairly deadened by vanity, all successive downward steps come easily enough. If a necklace be wanting, a necklace must be got; honestly, if one can, but got.

On the landing of the second floor stands, as we know, the life-sized figure of a saint, martyred, satin-slippered, glittering with gorgeous paste adornments. If the good old Beata would only lend that necklace of her's for half an hour, ten minutes, long enough to yield one some faint foretaste of the sweets of brilliants. If—assuming her permission—one were to borrow it, say! The glass-case can be opened by a cunning hand from the back: this fact, Belinda discovered when the first-floor lodger presented the saint with a new laced handkerchief at Easter. And no living soul is about; and it could not, surely, be much of a sin considering that the saint is but a big wax doll with bead eyes . . . and indeed if it were sin, is it not all-important, Mr. Jones and his suit impending, for Belinda to ascertain practically, whether diamonds are becoming to the complexion, and so worth the sacrifice of a life or not?

She creeps down the echoing stone stairs; her heart beating, her unaccustomed feet entangling themselves at every movement in her trailing skirt; she reaches the landing of the second floor. There stands the Beata, her livid hands crossed on her breast, her bead eyes awfully wide open. There are the paste brilliants. A struggling moonbeam rests on them; they glitter with deathly, horrible fascination. Belinda's heart and courage wax chill.

Suppose the outraged saint should come some night, and, standing beside her bed, lay an icy retributive hand upon her face! To meddle with these holy persons' beads, for aught she knows, may be the most mortal of crimes, and—"Crime, or no crime, *I will do it!*" decides the girl with the spasmodic coward's courage of her sex. Now, may fortune be her friend! May no inmate of the house pass from floor to floor while the sacrilegious act is being carried into effect.

The cranky fastening of the glass door gives a groan as she opens it, causing Belinda's guilty conscience to quake again; but no ear save her own hears the sound. She unclasps the necklace, shivering as her fingers come in contact with the clammy wax throat, then bears away her booty, her legs trembling under her at every step, upstairs. She takes it to the light of her solitary candle; admires its mock effulgence; clasps it, trembling, round her little warm soft neck; surveys herself on tip-toe in the tarnished mirror above the chimney-piece. And where is conscience, now, where remorse? Admirable monitors of men, the moment possession has brought satiety, why is it that Conscience and Remorse hold their peace as long as the taste of the apple continues sweet between our teeth!

She surveys herself, well nigh awe-stricken by her own fairness. She feels that to be the possessor of real diamonds she would cheerfully become Mrs. Augustus Jones and start for Clapham to-morrow. Now, nothing is wanting but a fan and lovers. The fan can be had; a huge gilt and black structure, of the date of thirty years ago, which lies, for ornament, on the mantelshelf; and of this Belinda possesses herself. But the lovers? Bah! some unimportant details are sure to be wanting at every rehearsal! When the prologue is over, the play played out in earnest, the lovers, it may be supposed, will come of themselves.

She struts up and down the room, her train outstretched, her fan in motion, her eyes glancing complacently at the mignon little figure the glass gives her duskily back. "If Captain Temple could see me—if Captain Temple could see me now!" thinks vanity. "If he knew I could be anything but ragged, and hideous, and a gamin." "And if he did know this, what would Captain Temple care?" says another sterner voice than that of vanity. "Of what account is the whole world to him by the side of Rose and Rose's beauty?"

A sudden leaden weight sinks dead on Belinda's heart. She is nothing to Roger Temple; holds no more place in his present than in his future. She seems to stifle. The saint's paste diamonds must, surely, be too heavy, so painful is the choking feeling in her throat. Turning abruptly away from the sight of her finery and of herself, she extinguishes the candle; then goes out, bare-armed, bare-necked, in her diamond necklace and train, upon the balcony.

It is now past midnight, and something like cooler air begins to stir across the sleeping country. Balmy sweet is the air; every floor of the vast old house has its balcony, every balcony its flowers; the sky is all a quiver with stars; mountains, river, plains, are lying in one great hush of purple sleep. Belinda rests her arm against the iron balustrade, and gazing away westward, towards the rugged line of Spanish coast, muses.

Spain or Clapham?

She has learnt much since she asked herself the same question this afternoon; unknowingly has passed the traditional brook, perhaps, where womanhood and childhood meet : for very certain has accepted Mr. Jones, elected in cold blood for Clapham : Clapham, respectability, riches. And yet—and yet, if Maria José (or some one else) were to appear before her just now, and——

Click, click, goes the sharp sound of a vesuvian, close, as it seems, beside Belinda's ear. She turns with a start, and there, on the adjoining balcony, *en robe de chambre*, and placidly lighting his midnight pipe of peace, stands Roger Temple. Roger may breakfast with Rose, dine with Rose, walk with Rose, spend any number of hours during the day that he chooses alone with Rose; but it would be the acme of indiscretion for him to lodge under the same roof with her. Thus the widow, well versed in the minutiæ of surface morals, decides. And so—from Scylla to Charybdis—fate and the landlord of the Hôtel Isabella together, have contrived to lodge him under the same roof with Belinda. The Maison Lohobiague has two flights of stairs—in these modern times has indeed been converted into two distinct houses, one of which is rented by the people of the "Isabella" as a succursale, or wing for overflowing guests, during the bathing season.

Belinda sees him, grasps the whole dramatic capabilities of the situation in a moment, but gives no sign. I have said that nature has endowed the child with abundant imitative talent; everyday association with the Basques, the most excitement-seeking, play-loving people in Europe, has stimulated the talent into a kind of passion. Now, she feels, is a magnificent opportunity for her to act, and with a purpose. A glance at Roger Temple's face convinces her that he does not recognize Rosie's vagrant out-at-elbows stepdaughter under the disguise of civilisation. Now she will have a rare opportunity of arriving at a truth or two ; now may she even test the practical worth of a "lifelong fidelity," see if this devoted lover cannot be led into a passing flirtation—moonlight, loneliness, the certainty of the crime remaining undetected, favouring

With an assumption of unconsciousness the most perfect, she resumes her former attitude, and, after a minute or two of silence, sings, in that undertone for which we have no word in English—the whisper of singing—a stanza of the mendicant student serenade, familiar from one end of the Peninsula to the other

> "Desde que soy estudiante,
> Desde que llevo manteo,
> No he comido mas que sopas
> Con suelas de zapatero."

She has a sweet, a sympathetic voice, *in posse*, like the beauty of her face ; and melody and voice alike harmonise deliciously with every external accessory of the scene.

"Brava, brava ! " exclaims Roger when she had finished. "That first verse was so excellently sung that it makes me eager for the second."

Belinda, thus unceremoniously accosted, turns upon him in all the conscious virtue of a trained dress and paste necklace.

"Señor ! " she exclaims, holding her head up with dignity, and in such a position that the moon shines upon its soft young outline full.

"I beg a thousand pardons," says Roger, putting his pipe hastily out of sight. "But the señora's song was so charming, I forgot that we had no master of the ceremonies to introduce us. Has it not a second verse ? "

"My song has a second and a third verse," replies Belinda, in English, strongly flavoured with Castilian gutturals. "I must acquaint his lordship, however, that I believed myself to be alone. I never sing for the pleasure of strangers, except when I am on the stage."

"The stage!" repeats Roger Temple, scrutinising the girlish face and figure critically. "Why, is it possible?"

"I have acted as long as I can remember," says Belinda, with all the effrontery conceivable. "If his English excellency has travelled through any of the principal Spanish towns he must have heard me."

"When the señora favours me with her name, I shall be able to question my memory more accurately," answers Roger.

Belinda pauses for a minute or two; then, "My name on the stage is Lagrimas," she tells him; "or, as you would say it in English, 'Tears.' Doleful, is it not? But I do not wish it changed. Who would not sooner be called Tears than Laughter?"

She sighs, and, half turning from him, rests her cheek down upon the graceful, bare arms that lie folded on the balcony. Seen thus in the moonlight, her bright hair falling around her shoulders, her childish face grown pensive, she seems to Roger as fair a little creature as ever blessed man's vision in this prosaic world; and his pulse quickens. The balconies are distant about four or five feet from each other. Leaning across the giddy intervening space, two persons of steady nerves might easily clasp hands, or, at least, touch fingers, if they were so minded. They are alone together, he and this girl— absolutely alone, as were the first pair of lovers in Eden; and yet impassably divided, as their lives are destined, in very fact, to be, for evermore. And Roger's pulse quickens.

During a great many years in India, I believe firmly

8

(without endorsing Rose's sentimentalities in general) that the image of his first-love did blind Roger Temple to most other women's attractions. But that was during the lifetime of the successive husbands, his rivals; while his passion remained hopeless, theoretic, intangible. Free, he continued faithful; bound—well, we will not say that his fidelity for a moment runs any serious danger, but he is undeniably more open to alien impressions than he used to be in his Indian days. Every man living, above the level of the savage, has a craving after contrast, as strong, pretty nearly, as the mere physical ones for food and drink. In India, Rose Shelmadeane, the modest flower-faced Rose of his imagination, was his contrast, the delightful ideal reverse; to all the women he lived amongst. Now, alas! now, every woman who is fresh and natural, who does not wear pearl-powder, does not demand tawdry compliments as a right, possesses for Roger Temple all the fatal charm of antithesis.

"Your philosophy is beyond your years, señora. Surely nothing should seem so good as laughter in one's youth."

"Youth!" echoes Belinda, raising her head quickly, and forgetting the Spanish accent and her assumed character together. "What have I to do with youth, Sir? When was I young? Why, from the time I was thirteen—"

And then her eyes meet Roger's, full, full in the moonlight. She stops and droops her face, crimsoning.

"Plenty of hard training has come to me in my life, señor," she goes on after a space, but without lifting her eyes again to his. "Sometimes I feel, a little too keenly, how well my name of Lagrimas fits me. But why should I talk of such things to-night? You know my country, Spain?" turning to him with the most irresistible of all coquetry, the coquetry that is born of ignorance. "No,

Well, you should run down there some day, now that you are so near. I will be your guide, if you choose."

"Done!" says Roger gaily. "It is a bargain that we take a Spanish tour together, Señora Lagrimas, is it not?"

"I don't think I said anything about 'together,' did I? But never mind that. Yes, we can go down to Granada first, if you like. It will take us a good week to see the Alhambra, and then—but is his excellency quite sure," pointedly, "that his time is his own?—that his friends will give him leave of absence?"

"Oh, no question of that," says Roger, with the airy assurance of an unfettered man. "The doubt is, rather, will the Señora Lagrimas keep her promise?"

"No question of that! Ready, after three minutes' temptation, to be led captive by the first strolling actress who accosts him from a balcony! So much for engaged men," thinks Belinda. "'So much for the romance of two young hearts, the fidelity of a lifetime,' et cetera. Let us try this devoted lover of Rose's a little further."

"I mentioned your friends, señor, because I know that you are not alone here. You may not have noticed me, but I certainly saw you to-night at the casino with ladies."

Roger Temple looks the very picture of innocence. "At the casino?" he repeats. "With ladies? Ah, to be sure, I believe I did speak to some English acquaintances of mine for a few minutes."

"There was an ugly little girl, for one—a girl very sunburnt, very ill-drest; you danced a waltz with her; and another lady, not so young. Your mamma, probably, señor?"

"Stepmamma," assents Roger, unblushingly, "and the stepmamma, also, of the little sunburnt girl with whom I danced."

"Consequently, you and the girl are—"

"Ah, that is a knotty point—the precise relationship between that young lady and myself. I will not allow you to call her ugly, though, Señora Lagrimas. Sunburnt she is; ill-drest she may be; ugly, never."

"Well, for my part, I do not see a good feature in the young person's face," says Lagrimas, with a contemptuous shrug of her shoulders. "A skin like a gipsy's, a wide mouth, a low forehead."

"Magnificent eyes and eyelashes, teeth like ivory, graceful little hands and feet, and the sweetest smile, when she chooses to smile, in the world."

"I should think her a vile temper, judging by her expression, and as to her manners—I have been here some time, señor—I know the girl by sight and by reputation. She plays boys' games with boys; robs henroosts after dusk with that dog of her's; she talks—swears, some people will tell you—like a gamin of the streets, and—"

"And for each and all of these small oddities I like her the better," interrupts Roger warmly. "Belinda is just the kind of girl to grow into the most charming of women in time."

"A charming woman! After the pattern of the other lady, who is not so young, the stepmamma?"

"No; not after that pattern, precisely, señora. Your vast experience must have taught you, surely, that there are more kinds of charming women in the world than one. Belinda has been neg . . . allowed to run a little too wild, hitherto; but circumstances, I am happy to say, will place her under my guidance now."

("Will they? will they, indeed, Captain Temple?" interpolates Belinda, mentally. "We shall see more about that by-and-bye.")

"She will live in my house, will stand to me in the position of a daughter, and I mean to reform her."

"Ah, heavens, how praiseworthy! How Christian!

Reform Belinda? With the aid of a severe English governess and a staff of attendant pastors and masters, of course?"

"Well, no," answers Roger. "I have no great belief in severe English governesses, neither are pastors or masters very much more to my taste. I shall reform Belinda, as much as she needs reforming, by kindness alone. It strikes me that what the poor little girl wants is, not sternness, but love."

Belinda turns her head away with a jerk: her throat swells, the big tears rise in her eyes. If he had said anything but this—if he had called her ugly, wicked, any hard name he chose, she could have borne it better.

"Belinda should be extremely grateful for your—your pity," she remarks, as soon as she can command her voice enough to speak. "For my part, I don't in the least value that kind of regard."

"No? And what kind of regard do you value, may I ask?" says Roger Temple, his tone softening.

"Ah—what kind? When I have known you a little longer than ten minutes I will tell you."

"The day we visit the Alhambra together, for instance?"

"Perhaps. Meantime, in Belinda's name, I thank you a thousand times for the *pity* you are charitable enough to bestow upon her. Good-night, señor. I leave you to think over your fine projects of reformation alone."

And with a mocking reverence "Lagrimas" salutes him; then, assuming the air of a princess, at least, and with a grand sweep of her rustling silken train, leaves the balcony.

She quits him, I say, with the air of a princess; the moment she is out of sight, turns, peeps through a rent in the dilapidated venetian blind, listens with eager, breathless curiosity to find out what Roger Temple will do next.

Captain Temple for a minute or two keeps silence. Then "Señora—Señora Lagrimas," he cries, softly.

But no answer comes to his appeal.

"Only one word—do you live here? Is there any chance of my seeing you again to-morrow night?"

Belinda is mute as fate.

"I shall listen for your voice towards eleven o'clock. If you do not take pity on me, I shall remain out here all night, remember, heart-broken."

"So much for engaged men, I say," thinks Belinda. "Oh, if I was really wicked, if I was half as bad as they give me credit for, could we not have a comedy in earnest out of all this?"

She retreats towards the middle of the room, and under voice sings another verse of the serenade.

> "Es tanta la hambra que tengo,
> Que ahora mismo me comiera,
> Los hierros de ese balcon,
> Y el cuerpo de mi morena!"

Then she steals back to the window to listen, her heart beating till she can hear its beats, her very finger-tips tingling with excitement, so carried away is she by this rôle of temptress that she is playing, the most fascinating rôle (save one, perhaps), of the whole little repertory of woman's life.

"The balconies are not very far apart, señora," remarks Roger, presently. "It would be quite possible for a desperate man to leap from one to the other."

A half-suppressed malicious laugh is the señora's only reply to this thrilling suggestion.

"I shall certainly make the attempt before long, and if I fail—mind, if I fall and am drowned, stifled, rather, in the harbour mud below, my death" (plaintively) "will be upon your conscience."

A laugh, rather more malicious, rather louder than before, is her reply.

"Señora Lagrimas! For the last time, will you or will you not come out and speak to me?"

And once more Belinda's silence says "No."

"I give you three chances. Señora Lagrimas!"

Silence.

"Lagrimas!"

Silence.

"Belinda, my dear!"

She flashes out upon him like a storm-wind; her lips apart, her eyes gleaming so that they eclipse the saint's diamonds on her throat.

"You—you dare to say you recognized me all the time?" This she asks him as soon as her indignation gives her breath to speak.

"I recognized you all the time," Roger confesses, humbly. "I knew you when I was lighting my pipe; I believe, before you saw me at all. Why in the world, should I not recognize you, my dear child?"

"Because I had been fool enough to disguise myself under this rubbish." With a fierce little gesture she apostrophizes Miss Burke's fine silk. "Because—oh! if I had known—if I could have guessed that you, of all people, would see me! And the nonsense you talked, Sir, the nonsense you dared to talk, knowing it to be me!"

"We have been talking very pleasantly," answers Roger Temple. "I cannot say I remember talking any particular nonsense."

"What! not when you told me, to my face, that circumstances had put me under your guidance; that you meant to reform me. *You*, to reform *me!*"

"It was a rash speech, I admit; I am not so sure that it was nonsense."

"And then our tour in Spain; but you shall keep to that —you shall keep to that, Captain Temple! Whatever Rose says, and whether the scheme is up to the Miss Ingram standard of propriety, or beneath it, I mean to hold you to your word. We are going to spend a week in Granada together, you and I."

"Of course, Rosie with us. What could be pleasanter? Rosie with us, and —"

"And Augustus Jones, too, if you please," interrupts Belinda, a curiously abrupt transition in her voice. "In the selfishness of your own happiness, you and Rose, you seem entirely to forget other peoples'. I go nowhere without Augustus, now."

"'Without Augustus,'" repeats Roger, blankly. "Why, Belinda, is it possible—can you mean —"

"I mean that I will go nowhere without Mr. Jones. Now, come, Captain Temple, or, as we are discussing family matters, let me call you by a sweeter future name—come now, step-papa, don't pretend. No concealment between near and dear relatives. As if you and Rosie did not know everything about my poor Augustus, just as well as I do!"

"I should be verry sorry to know one thing," says Roger, culpably negligent of his future matchmaking duties as a parent. "I should be very sorry to know that you cared seriously, young, ignorant of life as you are, for a person like —Jones!" It seems as though the obnoxious monosyllable would nearly choke him.

"Care! And, pray, who said anything about caring. Sir? I am going to *marry* Mr. Jones—we settled the whole affair to-night—marry, not care for him."

Marry, not care for him! As much repulsion as a man can feel, theoretically, towards a distractingly, pretty little girl, not five feet distant from him in the moonlight, Roger feels at this moment towards Belinda O'Shea. Rose was right. The Vansittart blood runs in her veins, poor child, and the blood is bad! Scarce seventeen yet, and she has the cold, mercenary instincts of a woman of thirty, and not by any means a good woman of thirty, either!

"You are slow with your congratulations; and the match is really a desirable one, step-papa—not, of course, for a moment speaking of Augustus personally. Bran-new villa at Clapham—if he does leave out a few of his H's, poor fellow, he makes up amply for them with his R's—villar at Clapham, opera-box, diamonds. My appearance is greatly improved by diamonds, is it not?" holding up a pendant of the saint's necklace between her fingers.

"Certainly. What lily is not improved by a little paint? All that glittering finery is Mr. Jones's first offering, I presume?"

"No," answers Belinda, calmly. "There has not been time, I am sorry to say, for offerings yet. He walked home with me after I left you and Rose at the Casino (poor Augustus felt, as I did, that our company was not wanted), and I invited him in, merely to keep me company whilst I ate my supper. And he proposed."

"He proposed. And you—"

"Accepted him, step-papa—what else should I do? And then, when I was alone again, the thought struck me of borrowing Burke's Sunday silk, just to see how I liked the taste of fine clothes; and I stole this necklace, Sir, from the throat of the old Beata who lives on our second landing—a paste necklace only, not real diamonds, such as I shall have when I am Mrs. Augustus Jones! Was it wicked, I wonder?" Sudden compunction for the sacrilege she has committed coming back upon her. "Captain Temple, do you think, now, the blessed old saints, when they are once safe in heaven, ever trouble themselves about the jewels they have left behind them on earth?"

Roger is silent. Belinda's worldliness has repulsed him to such a degree that he can no longer smile at her rattling talk; and still she fascinates him more and more. Girlish she is not: deliberately, in cold blood, has she not sold herself to a man she despises, openly glorying in the bargain?

Feminine she is not: right well can he imagine those eyes of hers flashing, those lips quivering, with the fierce excitement of a bull-fight. Innocent she is not: witness the stories she told them at the Casino, the gusto with which, ten minutes ago, she sustained her part of Lagrimas. And still, devoid though she be of every virtue that can be catalogued, there is in her a charm more potent than all the cardinal virtues put together. Some few exceptional people exist in this world who are a law unto themselves; people endowed with that rarest of gifts, the fine flower of prefect originality, and whose qualities are not to be measured out by the common foot-rule of good and evil. Belinda is one of them. And Roger Temple, cruel malice of fate, is precisely the man to appreciate the wild, bitter-sweetness of her character to the uttermost. Men of his semi-poetic stamp fall in love often with conventional dolls, as he has done; marry conventional dolls, as he will do; and, pathetically conscious that the nearest relations of their lives have been incomplete, go to their grave without tasting the nectar of true passion once, for sheer lack of opportunity. But let opportunity come! Let a woman, fresh and faulty from Nature's hand, cross their path—

Well, our little story of elective affinities has not progressed as far as that yet. Roger is engaged to Rose, Belinda to Mr. Jones; and Belinda and Roger are nothing to each other, for one more quarter of an hour, at all events.

They talk on and on, and presently Augustus is forgotten, and presently, Rose. Belinda is Lagrimas again, and Roger the wandering Englishman who has fallen but too quickly a victim to Lagrimas' charms. By-and-bye the air, all at once, grows fresh; a flicker of pink light begins to show above the glorious chain of mountain-peaks towards the east; and, with a start, Belinda realizes that it is morning—that Miss Burke will be back before noon, that Roger is the lover of

Rose, and that she has decided to spend her life at Clapham with Mr. Augustus Jones!

"Captain Temple, do you know that the sun is going to rise, that we have been out here since midnight, you and I? I hope you never mean to talk of reforming me again. Oh, if Rose knew! Shall you tell her?"

"Shall you tell Mr. Jones, Belinda?"

And then their eyes meet, with a sweet sudden look of intimacy—they have been acquainted now near upon a dozen hours—and the girl questions him no more.

They bid good-bye and part; the tacit promise exchanged, though no word of promise be spoken, of seeing each other at the same place and time to-morrow night. And then, left alone to conscience and tobacco, Roger Temple, it may be hoped. feels some misgivings as to the wisdom of his first attempt at reformation, some doubts as to the safety of this close neighbourhood of balconies. As for Belinda—Belinda has passed her seventeen years of life, reader, in a moral atmosphere unfavourable to the development of casuistic niceties, and she is simply in a seventh heaven of happiness. Really in love with Roger Temple, after one night's flirtation on a balcony, she is not; but she is in the state dangerously apt to precede real love in a very young and very natural girl's heart. Vanity sweetly flattered, imagination kindled, just the least little delightful thrilling sense of treading on thin ice aroused. Oh, blessed prudishness that made Rose banish him from beneath the roof of her hotel! Oh, blessed chance that sent him to a room and balcony in the Maison Lohobiague! Stealing to the dusky mirror, she smiles at her own image in the day-dawn, unwillingly loosens the half-dead passion-flower from her hair, then, exchanging Miss Burke's training silk for her own shabby Cinderella frock, creeps down to the second floor with the borrowed brilliants, and actually gives the saint's cold hand a kiss of gratitude as she replaces them.

Poor good old Beata, shut away in her glass-case from moonlight, flower-scents, handsome faces—from all the pleasant things we still enjoy, and sin through, in the flesh! Something in the peculiar waxy flavour of the hand carries Belinda back, in remembrance, to the days of the Irish convent, when her highest reward for any exceptional good conduct was to be held aloft and allowed to salute the fingers or toes of some glass-encased beatitude. The remembrance leads on to another. At the end of the convent garden, sheltered by thickest growing wych-elms, was a certain walk from whence could be seen through iron railings the world —the wicked outer world of men and women, passing along one of the smaller streets of Cork. None of the small children were ever allowed to tread that walk, and to deter them thence the old French nun, who watched their play, used to speak of it, beneath her breath, as "le bout du monde." No good little girl could surely wish to go to the "bout du monde!" And Belinda did wish it passionately, and though she obeyed the letter of the injunction through love, her highest, only law, never ceased to gaze with longing eyes towards the spot whose forbidden imagined delights rendered all the legitimate garden walks so tasteless.

Does the same taint of the primeval sin lurk in her heart still?

When she returns upstairs, she peeps once more through the dilapidated venetian at her neighbour's balcony; she smells the odour of his pipe, muses awhile on Lagrimas, Granada, Alhambra—her "bout du monde," now . . . .

And then she goes to her pillow and dreams, not of any perplexing *meum* and *tuum*, not of Rose's lover, not of her own; but of boleros, bull-fights, hen-roost robbing with Costa, and similar every-day diversions of her vagabond life.

CHAPTER IX.

THE FINGER OF FATE.

Rose is a woman of whom it may be fairly said that to love her is a liberal education—in folly.

Roger Temple finds his acquirements in this valuable branch of knowledge ever steadily increasing. Leaving her of an evening, in as deadened a state of brain as the utterances of a beloved object can possibly induce, it seems to him, at times, that even Rose can never astonish him more on the score of unreason. And lo, next morning, she startles him with some new outbreak, some fresh vagary of millinery, mind or morals, that leaves all past ones far behind!

Upon a clever woman, a good woman, a wicked woman, a man may, in some measure, count; upon a foolish one, never. Folly, a certain pitch attained, seems inexhaustible as genius itself; possibly, if mental qualities, like material ones, could be subjected to scales and crucible, might prove to be genius, of some spurious or bastard kind. Especially in aught that ministers to personal vanity is this inexhaustibleness patent. Women, you may find in plenty, who believe one man, two men, twenty men, to be their victims. Rose is ready, on the weakest evidence, or on no evidence at all, to believe it of the universe. Borne on the strong pinion of vanity, she can even rise to being imaginative, as the sequel of this history will show.

"You would never guess what has happened, Roger, never! And I am not at all sure that I am wise to tell you, you naughty, naughty, jealous man—only when he comes it may be worse!"

It is noon next day; and in Rose's cool, Moorish-looking drawing-room at the "Isabella," the lovers are love-making: the widow in an embroidered India muslin wrapper (one of the eight becoming morning-dresses she has brought with her from London), and as coy, and coquettish and playful of demeanour as any youthful bride of eighteen.

"If it will ease your conscience to make confession, I promise solemnly to restrain my jealousy," says Roger; not, it may be presumed, without some uneasy conscience-twinges of his own. "You have made another conquest, Rose?"

The droop of Mrs. O'Shea's eyelids says yes.

"I was sure of it. That little Portuguese Jew at breakfast—no, the Spanish officer last night at the Casino! Rose, if it is that good-looking Spanish scoundrel—"

"Oh, Roger, don't be violent! How can I help men being so ridiculous?—I, who never give anyone any encouragement! No, it is neither the Spaniard nor the Portuguese—I mean it is some one else as well. Oh, I do feel so guilty! I'm sure these things never happen to any one but me."

"I dare say they happen to most pretty women," says Roger. He seldom lets go an opportunity of administering the expected lump of sugar to the widow's lips. "But put me out of my torture. Who is my latest rival, Rosie?"

"Well, you must know, dear, Spencer went to the post-office this morning, and there was a letter for me."

"It was a declaration."

"It was from cook. I left orders with her to write regularly every week—and indeed, a friend of Spencer's is staying in the house as a precaution. I never like to doubt the honesty of the lower classes, Roger, and of course you cannot make away with tables and chairs, still there are the clocks and the ornaments, and as to house linen—"

"But my rival, Rosie, my rival? While you talk about the cook and the house linen, I am burning with impatience, remember."

For once, at least, during his courtship, Roger Temple contrives to unite veracity with sweetness.

"Well, it seems he called very soon after we left. 'A tall, military-looking gentleman, with a moustache,' cook says, 'and would take no denial, but walked in as if the place was his own,'—those are exactly her words—'and looked particularly hard at the photograph of Captain Temple in the breakfast-room.' Ah, Roger, what he must have suffered! Well, I know what he must have suffered at that moment!"

"What who must have suffered, my love? The end of the story is, naturally, that cook searched for the tea-spoons, on the military gentleman's departure, and found them missing."

"The end of the story is nothing of the kind," says Rose, fluttering up her feathers like a little sparrow. "The end of the story is that cook gave him my address here—and I am afraid told him *other news* that made him most unhappy —and he said he should follow me straight to St. Jean de Luz. I call that something like constancy, poor fellow! Although he must have known the hopelessness of his position, to resolve, without a moment's hesitation, upon following me."

"Other people, knowing the hopelessness of their position, have remained constant to you, Rose," says Captain Temple, tenderly.

(Does it flash across his mind that fidelity seems to be more closely allied with the state of hopelessness than with that of hope?)

"And now I shall have you both upon my hands at once. And I am sure he is of the most *fiery*, combative temperament—those glowering, deep-set, eyes that give a man such a look of Power, and beautiful long auburn moustache, and six feet one at least," adds Rose, with a reproachful glance at her lover's inferior stature.

"Rosie," says Roger, with a thoroughly sincere sigh, " do you want to drive me clean out of my senses? Who is he? Deep-set eyes, auburn moustache, Power, and six feet one! I cannot endure it, Rosie. There are limits remember, even to my long-suffering."

Rose dimples, and colours, and casts her eyelids up and down, as, all unsuspicious of latent irony, she drinks in this flattery which is the very meat and drink of her small soul.

"It is Colonel Drewe, then, as you insist upon knowing. He refused, it seems, to give his name to the servants, but I—oh! there are intuitions that cannot be mistaken. It is Stanley Drewe."

"Drewe, Drewe—the lack-a-daisical old dandy, with a flower in his button-hole, whom you have got in your photograph book? You had a tremendous flirtation with Colonel Drewe once, my dear, had you not?"

"You would not blame me in that affair, Roger, if you knew all. You were far away in India—indeed, it was in poor Major O'Shea's lifetime: and I am sure his passions were so violent, I never dared look at any man twice. But whatever party I was seen at during one whole season, Colonel Drewe was certain to be there, too. If I went to the opera, I saw him. If I drove in the park, I saw him. It was an infatuation, and if I had been free—however, I was not free!" says Rose, in a tone of exquisite abnegation. "I was not free, and he behaved beautifully, poor Stanley! He went to Gibraltar with his regiment, and we have corresponded a little since; only the other day, indeed,

I sent him an announcement of Uncle Robert's death. What a blow this must be to him?"

A look not so much of anger as of pain passes over Roger Temple's face. He may have ceased to be enamoured of Rose; he has not ceased to be enamoured of his own ideal love for her; the love which, wise or foolish, in itself, has for a dozen years been part and parcel of his life. For the sake of that, not because of the *fade* flirtation of these two elderly London butterflies, he feels wounded.

"A blow to Colonel Drewe! What—our engagement Rosie? Had matters gone so far between you, then, that Colonel Drewe has a right to consider your marrying another man than himself 'a blow?'"

"Ah! Roger, dearest, I implore you not to be angry! How can I control poor Stanley's feelings? I declare, between you all, I don't know which way to turn. And now to think of the dreadful embarrassment of having him here!"

"As far as I am concerned, there will be none whatsoever," answers Roger, coldly. "You and Colonel Drewe, of course, know best what reason you have for embarrassment."

He is annoyed, lowered for her sake, rather than his own. But Rose, who is no adept at reading the character of others, sets him down simply as "jealous" (a mistake into which vanity not unfrequently conducts intelligence of her calibre); and twitters on and on about poor Stanley's infatuation and deep-set eyes, and her own innocence, and the embarrassment of riches that awaits her in the way of admirers, until the very excess of her folly brings her lover back to good temper. Dear, simple-hearted little Rosie! Who can be angry with her long? Her vanities are so childlike, her flirtations, like her whole character, so transparent!

"You may be sure he rushed to England as soon as ever he got the news of Uncle Robert's death. I am not a fool, Roger, and I don't think myself quite hideous, but I know very well that men like to marry money, and that, in my small way, I am an heiress. Can't you fancy him looking round the house, *speculating?* And then to come upon your portrait! I wonder, now, whether it was quite proper of me to have it hung up yet? Nothing would pain me more than for Colonel Drewe to think me indelicate."

"We are certain, I suppose, that it is Colonel Drewe, Rosie? There is no one else among your numerous victims whom the cap could fit?"

Oh! yes, on this point Rosie is confident. If it had not been for the moustache it might have been the Reverend Roland Lascelles, whom she met last year at Malvern, the most elegant, the most spiritual-minded of men; but no—with a conscious little sigh over her Malvern reminiscences; the moustache settles it. Colonel Drewe it must be, and no other. "And what makes it the more remarkable, Roger," adds Rose, with her most sapient and logical air, "I declare it looks like the finger of fate—I dreamed of poor Major O'Shea only last night! It seemed some one in America had told him of my engagement—in dreams, alas! in dreams only, our dead are restored to us!—and he had brought me over the most lovely turquoise and pearl set as a wedding present (Major O'Shea always used to say how pearls became me!) and was exceedingly pleased at the marriage, and said he wished you joy from his heart. Was it not most remarkable?"

"Most remarkable and most unpleasant," answers Roger, getting annoyed in earnest. "For God's sake, Rose, dream no more dreams! Rivals of flesh and blood, powerful colonels, and elegant parsons, I can stand, not the others—"

But happily, at this very delicate juncture, the door opens; and the entrance of Belinda and Miss Burke puts an end to the love scene.

CHAPTER X.

"LAGRIMAS!"

Miss Lydia Burke is by no means an unfavourable sample, outwardly, of the Woman of the Future. She has a tolerable sandy complexion, tolerable sandy hair, teeth almost over white and even, and a pair of very wide-awake small grey eyes. Her walk is wiry; her figure like a bit of watch-spring; her age—the hitherward side of forty. What in this bright energetic-looking lady should have introduced the sad elements of hatred and disbelief into Belinda's young life? What has caused the inalienable discrepancies between them?

Mainly, I imagine, this unchangeable law; that reality and shams will no more mix together than will oil and water. Born of no super-honest stock, reared in no super-honest school, one virtue, from her earliest babyhood, took sturdy root in Belinda's soul—the virtue of absolute truth. Organisations exist, so finely-tempered that their possessors can detect the presence of certain flowers or animals, as if by instinct. Belinda is gifted with the same prescience, the same kind of moral divining wand, as regards imposture. And poor Miss Burke, while she for ever preaches Earnestness, Woman's Work, Woman's Mission (with big capitals), is an arch impostor; false, sham, to her finger tips! Not an uninteresting type to the philosophic student of character; but to an ignorant ardent mind like Belinda's, about as nauseating a specimen of human nature as our race can produce.

Ten, fifteen years ago, say the traditions of Eastern travellers, Miss Lydia Burke used to haunt the hotels of Egypt and Palestine. She was a prettyish woman then; prettyish, unprotected, and, though not a girl, young enough to be regarded with suspicion by ladies travelling under the legitimate wing of husbands or brothers. Perhaps there were no really queer stories about her—I mean, perhaps none of the queer stories about her had real foundation. That she was in the habit of borrowing money from any man who would lend her money is matter of fact. But in those days, it must be remembered, Miss Lydia Burke had projects of founding ragged Jew schools in the Levant. Who shall say that the loans did not go to ragged Jew schools in the Levant? Later on, she frequented the Alps; unprotected still; still short of money; an indomitable climber: Bloomerish in dress; rather less shunted by ladies than formerly—(alas, her prettiness was fading!) feared exceedingly by bachelor parties of young men, on whom under various pretexts, she was wont to fasten with a cruel and leech-like tenacity. After this—well, after this, Miss Burke wrote a book "My Experiences." Then, a little more Bloomerish, a little more faded, financial resources at a lower ebb than ever, turned up in London.

The book, a hash of doubtful Oriental narrative, and still more doubtful Exeter Hall piety, was simply below criticism; but, by one of those outside chances, occasionally to be met with in the world of writing as of men, it sold. It sold, and Miss Burke straightway manufactured a three-volume novel, carefully flavoured with the same kind of spice as before, but with the piety omitted, which did not sell. And then she became Earnest for life; shortened her skirts, had her jackets cut after the fashion of men's coats, wriggled her way, ere long, upon platforms, I think made a speech or two about female suffrage, and began in common conversation to speak of women as Woman. And it was just when she had reached this melancholy turning-point in the downward road that the advertisement in the *Times* brought Belinda O'Shea into her hands.

Finding herself a good deal snubbed by the leading members of the strong sisterhood in London—neophytes without cash are apt, in more sects than one, to be lightly looked upon by the elders—poor Burke had to consider how Earnestness could be made to pay, and in a happy moment of inspiration composed the advertisement that sealed Belinda's fate. And then commenced the adventuress life again on the Continent—the adventuress life, but with a difference!

Earnest English people, pious English people, all English people, as far as the writer has personally known or heard of, like to be connected with anything that is connected with an earl. Miss Burke liked exceedingly to be connected with the Earl of Liskeard's granddaughter, although, from the first moment Belinda's eyes looked her hollow soul through, she disliked the society of the child herself.

"The Honourable Belinda O'Shea and Miss Burke." So, during the early days of their wanderings, she invariably caused their names to be written in hotel books or on continental church lists, despite all Belinda's angry protests against the imposture. If they travelled in the same railway carriage with an Englishman, if they sat opposite an Englishman at breakfast or dinner, Miss Burke always contrived to trade upon him with her small companion's birth and parentage, and, with singularly few exceptions, found the venture answer. Belinda remembers still—bitterly, chokingly remembers, dinners and drives and theatre tickets presented to them, at that period, by chance table-d'hôte acquaintance, and of which she now knows her poor little forlorn aristocratic society must have been the price. Facts proving two things, reader: first, that Miss Burke had inborn aptitude for the money-raising or adventuress craft; secondly, that there are men in the world who will pay to shake hands with an earl's granddaughter, just as others will pay to see General Tom Thumb or the Two-headed Nightingale.

As time went on, Belinda, it need hardly be said, turned rebellious on this as on most other points. "I am not an Honourable, and I will not have you write me down one, madam. The earl, my grandpapa, has never seen me, does not mean to see me, does not acknowledge my existence. If you bring in his name before any of these commis-voyageurs again, I will tell them the truth."

And Miss Burke knew the sturdy, nothing-fearing nature of her charge too well to risk the experiment.

They never came to open or violent rupture. Belinda's money stood between Miss Burke and want. Miss Burke stood between Belinda and her stepmother. They detested each other, were necessary to each other, kept together. Is not a good half of the world for ever performing that same duo in this queer comedy of errors, this jumble of mistaken enforced companionships, that we call society?

"Poor little Belinda is so curiously frivolous, so thoroughly, constitutionally devoid of all seriousness of purpose," Miss Burke explains, whenever the subject seems to require self-extenuation. "But her health being delicate, her papa and mamma both in an early grave, I try to reconcile the out-of-door life she leads to my conscience."

"Burke is the out-and-outest impostor that ever walked," Belinda will say to her gamin friends. "I saw Tartuffe at the play once, and, by Heaven, he was nothing to her! What is she an impostor for? If I knew *that* I might detest her less. I believe the creature is false to her own conscience. I believe she dreams lies."

So things have gone on until they are as we see them now: Miss Burke collecting ideas for her great work on social reform, "The Woman of the Future;" Belinda running wild, neglected, as nearly on the road to ruin as was ever innocent, honest, little human soul, about the streets of St. Jean de Luz. The practical at war with the ideal, as we so often find to be the case in this imperfect world.

Nothing can be blander than the meeting between Belinda's stepmamma and her preceptress. Miss Burke has held religiously to the letter of the bargain sealed between them in London, has kept the girl conveniently out of Rosie's way during the past three years. Rosie has held to hers; each quarterly payment for maternal watchfulness and superior intellectual culture has been paid, in advance, without a question. They begin to talk platitudes. Rose thinks dear Belinda grown, though a little sunburnt. Miss Burke trusts dear Mrs. O'Shea has overcome the fatigues of travelling? A very wearying journey from London to St. Jean de Luz.

"Yes, indeed, especially when one is travelling alone with one's maid," cries Rose, sensitive ever as to the smaller proprieties, and virtuously conscious that she only "met" Roger Temple in Paris, Bordeaux, and elsewhere. "One does feel so miserably helpless without a gentleman."

"Well, for my part I see no use in them whatever," says Miss Burke. "When you are alone you have nothing but your luggage to look after. When you are burdened with a man," this with a depreciatory glance in the direction of Roger, "you have to look after him and your things too."

"My things!" exclaims Belinda, in her mocking voice. "Well, Miss Burke, in the present state of affairs my 'things' would not require much looking after, with a man, or without one. Do you know, ma'am," seriously, "the washerwoman says there is really nothing more of mine for her to bring back? The last remaining tatters I had have vanished—carried away by the birds, I suppose, to build their nests."

She perches herself in her accustomed favourite place, the corner of the table, and looks round cheerfully on the company, as she volunteers this information.

A cold glitter comes into Burke's eye. "You are almost of an age, I must say, Miss O'Shea, to begin to care for order. No achievement in life can be ever made without order. When I was seventeen I had no greater delight than in the neat arrangement of my wardrobe."

"But I have no wardrobe to keep neat, ma'am. Wardrobe! Why, this is my only frock; and as to stock—"

"Belinda, my dear Belinda, you forget. Another time," interrupts Rose, colouring, "What have you been doing with yourself to-day, my love? And last night. Did Mr. Jones see you safe home? I had a note from him this morning, saying he had gone off to the mountains, and that I must ask you for particulars. Now, what does it all mean?"

She frisks over like a little lambkin to her stepdaughter's side, and putting her arm round her waist—Belinda holding herself uncompromisingly stiff under the caress—begins to gush and titter, school-girl fashion, in her ear. Miss Burke and Roger are thus left to make conversation for each other.

"A very interesting country this, Sir," observes the lady, looking sourly at Roger's handsome face. Sourly—oh, Miss Burke, you, who, fifteen years ago could look at no man without a melting smile! But such are the results of Earnestness. "Interesting, I mean, to those who visit it with a Purpose."

"Yes; I am told you get very fair snipe-shooting here in winter," answers Roger, who does not understand the argot of Miss Burke's sect.

"I speak of the inhabitants, sunk now in superstition, but the remnants of a noble race. You are, perhaps, no

aware that the Basque has outlived five distinct peoples?—
the Carthaginians, Celts, Romans, Goths, and Saracens."

("Murray," says Belinda, in a stage whisper. "'Introductory Remarks on the Pyrenees,' page two hundred and forty-nine.")

Roger strokes his moustache and tries to look edified. "The Basque must certainly be very old," he begins, foolishly.

"But the work that I am engaged on at present—the work that, indeed, fills every moment of my time, in the search of illustration. You have perhaps heard, through Miss O'Shea, that I am writing a book? No? I might have guessed as much. Miss O'Shea's interests do not lie in the direction of my own. A book entitled 'The Woman of the Future.' I am a labourer, Sir, though a humble one, in the greatest reformation of our day—the work of restoring Woman to the pedestal from whence the blinded prejudices of centuries have dethroned her.''

"Ah, yes," says Roger, in no very enthusiastic tone, and glancing, as he speaks, at the patches where darns ought to be on Belinda's stockings. "For my part," he adds gallantly, "I cannot see that any reformation is needed. It seems to me that women are exceedingly charming as they are."

"As the Turk, as the Debased Asiatic thinks of his slaves," cries Miss Burke. "The age has passed, Sir, for such cheap chivalry. Do you, an Englishman, actually advance the proposition that 'to be charming' is a fit motive for an immortal being's existence?"

"The most charming women appear to me to be so without any motive at all," says Roger, mentally measuring the distance between his adversary and the door. "But I am really the worst fellow living at an argument."

"Oh! that is a very easy way of escape. It is perfectly evident to what cynical school you belong—the surface light in which you regard our sex! Can you solemnly affirm, Sir,

I ask it with the earnestness the subject requires, that you do not look upon us as Toys?"

Thus put, as it were, upon oath, Roger Temple considers Miss Burke's personal attractions more closely than he has yet done—the thin cold features, the glistening eyes, the watch-spring figure. He feels that he does not, that in his wildest moments he never could look upon her in the obnoxious light she deprecates, and with a perfectly clear conscience answers, "No."

"Then may I ask what *do* you look upon us as?" says Burke, pitilessly.

Roger not only measures the distance between himself and the door, he rises to his feet. He has been held a brave soldier in action, a hardy sportsman in the field; but he is horribly afraid of Miss Lydia Burke. "I—I really beg pardon—but I have usually looked upon women as women," he answers, humbly.

Miss Burke turns her head away in contempt.

"It really is most wonderful," sighs Rose, who has caught the last word or two of the discussion, "most extraordinary, how gentlemen do dislike intellect in us! I am sure, for myself, I envy superior women, and I have always wished and wished to be blue; haven't you, Belinda?"

"I like my natural hue well enough, Rose," answers the girl pertly. "Still, if I were forced to change, I believe I would as soon be blue as some other colours. Superior women do not usually wear rouge or pearl-powder, do they?" She looks more thoroughly hard, more deliberately, elfishly wicked than ever, as she implants this savage little stab. Alas! where are all the budding graces, where is the soft, shy dawning womanliness of the "Lagrimas" of last night?

"But must your choice, of necessity, lie between the two?" Roger asks, in that quiet tone of his which at once softens and exasperates her. "Are blue and rouge the only two colours in the world?"

"Certainly they are not, Captain Temple. There is sun-tan, for instance; Vandyck brown; the fine natural colour of gamins, beggars, gipsies, and all the great unwashed of nature—my colour."

"Unwashed! You quite pain me with these expressions, Belinda," says Rose. "But you must try not to despair about your complexion, dear. Spencer shall make you some of her milk of roses. She got the receipt from Lady Harriet, and they say the effect is extraordinary; that sun-tan, and *even freckles* can be cured by it. For my part," encouragingly, " I have no great faith in cosmetics. You are fair or you are swarthy by constitution."

Her last fatal fancy about Colonel Drewe has melted poor Rosie into amiability towards the whole world, Belinda even included. So amiable, so elated is her frame of mind, that she has been rash enough to whisper her little budget of hopes and fears and projects into the girl's unsympathetic ear. "An old—ah, if she must confess truly, a dear friend—coming after her to St. Jean de Luz! Could anything be imagined more difficult than the part she would have to play? And Roger so jealous already; that is his weak point, you know, poor fellow, jealousy. And will Belinda find out where Spencer can buy one of those becoming Spanish combs and a mantilla?" For Rosie's imagination always flies to the millinery department, the stage properties of any coming event, as the imagination of a more highly-endowed woman might fly to what she should say, or feel, or dissemble. If the Colonel make his appearance of a morning, Rose has decided that she will receive him in white cashmere, ever so sparingly relieved by the palest shade of lavender ribbons; if at night, in a high Spanish comb, a lace veil, and jet cross. What *could* be more appropriate than a lace veil and jet cross to a lovely little widow, who is roaming about the world, breaking the heart of every ill-fated man she comes across

It is long before the visit draws to an end; and Captain, Temple, doubly guarded by Rosie and Miss Burke, does not exchange another syllable with Belinda. At last, in the middle of one of Miss Burke's finest perorations on Woman's Destiny, the girl brusquely takes her departure from the room, and accompanying her to the top of the hotel stairs, Roger gets a word or two with her alone.

"You are not going to play paume to-day?" for she has a racket-ball and schistera, as usual, in her hand. "Under this broiling sun! Belinda, I will not allow it."

"Will you not, indeed, Captain Temple? Why not, pray?"

"I do not choose you to spoil your complexion, for one thing."

"My unwashed complexion, that is to be improved by Lady Harriet's milk of roses! Isn't it *fine* to hear Rosie and Miss Burke talk? What advantages I have had, Sir, in being guided by those two extremes of feminine intelligence!"

"Promise me you will not play paume, Belinda, to-day, or any other day."

She hesitates and looks down; a quiver on her lip, a tell-tale blush shining beneath the clear olive of her cheek.

"Lagrimas!" he whispers softly; "will you promise?"

And then she raises her eyes. They promise; unconsciously, they promise a world too much to Roger Temple.

CHAPTER XI.

A TRANSFORMATION SCENE.

HAVE you watched an almond-tree flower? Bare, shivering boughs to-day—to-morrow, under the first warm kiss of April, a cloud of odorous luxuriant blossom. Such change, such sudden miracle of growth, is wrought during the next four days in Belinda. Her cheek gains colour, her figure roundness; her hair, no longer disfigured by the villanous plaits, hangs round her neck in waves of glossy chestnut. Her movements lose their masculine roughness, her dress grows neat. Girlish grace, girlish softness, modesty—all have come to her. Who shall unriddle these things?

"Belinda is not going to be so unfortunately plain, I do believe," Rose will remark complacently to her lover. "She has quite made up her mind to marry Mr. Jones—quite; and you see how she brightens up at the prospect of riches. I am afraid I was right about that poor thing from the first, Roger. Belinda has no heart."

Miss Burke accounts for the transformation otherwise. "A nature like Belinda's," says Miss Burke, "can only develope from one frivolity to another. Her childish love of play outgrown, and Belinda takes to—what? Earnest work, higher culture, recognition of the world's wants and miseries? No! To muslins, ribbons, and laces; the livery, the badge of woman's degradation in the social scale."

So think these ladies. What does Roger Temple think?

Roger Temple is in the frame of mind, reader, when we all of us are apt to shun self-communion, to keep the eyes of the spirit shut. By nature, the most chivalrously loyal of men, Roger is drifting, daily, hourly, drifting into disloyalty. He is more attentive, more devoted than ever to Rosie during the hours that he is at her feet—poor, unconscious Rosie, perpetually devising toilettes for Colonel Drewe, who as yet comes not. But there are a great many hours of the day when he is not at Rosie's feet. The adorers of mature beauty are generally debarred from adoration during the forenoon, that sacred, mysterious time for women to whom heaven hath given one face and who manufacture to themselves another. Till eleven or twelve o'clock every morning Roger is free, and Belinda also. After the casino ball at night he is free again, and then, in the starlight, "Lagrimas" steals out upon the balcony (so fatally near his own) of the Maison Lohobiague.

Miss Burke, absorbed in the "Woman of the Future," sees nothing. Rosie, enrapt in lavender ribbon, Spanish combs, and agitated suspense about that elegant creature Stanley, suspects nothing. And then, under this southern sky, in this do-nothing life, the path—no difficult one in any climate—that leads from flirtation to friendship, from friendship to a warmer feeling, is so easy. Conscience? Why, 'tis too hot in St. Jean de Luz for such compunctious visitings of nature. The mere act of existing is a lethe; a dream of sapphire skies and sapphire sea, of romance, music, passion-flowers on a balcony, and one exquisite girl's face shining from amidst them. Alas the pity, that to dreams so flattering sweet comes invariably awakening so substantial! Four glowing nightless days pass by like one, Miss Burke engaged philosophically, Rose making futile millinery preparation for Colonel Drewe, Roger Temple and Belinda falling about as desperately in love with each other as ever two people fell on this contradictory earth. For the fifth day Rosie has planned an eight-hours' excursion into Spain—Hendaye, Fontarabia, home through the mountain-pass of Behobia by moonlight. Mr. Jones is to return early in the morning from his tour, and, as a matter of course, will accompany them. "Two pairs of lovers! I never heard of anything so ridiculous," says Rosie. With Miss Burke, note-book in hand, as duenna, or fifth wheel of the coach.

Such is the day's plan; a plan, like the great Frederic's "fort beau sur le papier;" but destined to vary considerably from the original rough draft, as the fairest mortal projects do when reduced to the harsh reality of practice.

And in the first place, as regards Mr. Jones. Augustus arrives punctually by the early morning train from Bayonne, and with lover like ardour makes his way at once under the broiling sun to the Maison Lehobiague, where Belinda, already equipped for the day's excursion, meets him just outside the house. Forgotten Jones, during his absence, she has not, nor her own quasi encouragement of his suit, having indeed been pointedly reminded of both about six times during each twenty-four hours, by Rose. But just at this present moment, dressed, poor little girl, in a summer frock and hat that Spencer has condescendingly made up for her, a flower in her waist-belt, the sunshine that human lives know only once in its extremest brightness shining from every feature of her face—at this particular moment, I say, the sudden apparition of Augustus, more blistered than ever after his journey, more mosquito-bitten, more amative, comes upon Belinda with all the cold chill of an unexpected misfortune. She changes colour painfully, does not offer to take his outstretched hand, and can find no utterance of welcome more flattering, more lover-like, than the monosyllable, "You!"

"Me," says Mr. Jones, ungrammatically tender. "I

have not kept you waiting, I hope? You have not been expecting me long?"

"Expecting? Well, certainly not. I don't know that I expected you at all," answers Belinda, drily. "You have seen Rose?"

No; Augustus has not yet had that pleasure. He found a note from Mrs. O'Shea on his table, inviting him to accompany them for the day into Spain, and then—"then, of course, I rushed off at once to see *you*, Belinda," he adds, in tenderer accents than before. "Has time hung heavy on your hands?" Mr. Jones has an unhappy knack of composing sentences brimful of murdered aspirates. "Has your heart told you that—that some one you cared for a little was away during the last four days?"

"My time has not hung in the least heavily on my hands," answers Belinda, coldly emphasising every "h." "But I have been aware of your absence, if you mean that."

"And what have you been doing with yourself? No paume playing, I hope?"

"I have given up paume playing for ever," she exclaims, her cheeks glowing, a sudden shame coming into her eyes as she makes the confession.

"My dear Belinda—this delightful compliance with my wishes"—begins Augustus.

"Your wishes!" she interrupts him quickly. "What do you mean by that, Sir? What do you suppose your wishes have had to do in the matter?"

"A good deal, I should hope, considering how we stand to each other as—as engaged people, and that," says young Crœsus, purpling.

Belinda turns from him impetuously—she trifles with the flower in her belt; she stoops and pats Costa, who with an air of dignified triumph, sits in the sunshine, eyeing the discomfiture of his enemy askance.

"I did not think you would begin any of that ridiculous nonsense again, Mr. Jones," she remarks, after a minute's silence. "Engaged! What for, pray? Macaroons at Harranbour's? We shall have time enough to get some, I dare say, before we start for Spain."

Without answering a word, Jones shifts his position from one leg to the other, then stands critically gazing into the transparent girlish face before him. Wounded vanity has intuitions, keen as those of love itself; nay, in nine times out of ten, I would say, has intuitions that come a thousandfold straighter and swifter to the mark! Wounded vanity is flooding Mr. Jones's intelligence with a curious amount of light at this moment.

"I don't know how it is, but it seems to me that you have altered a good deal since I went away, Miss Belinda. Upon my word, you look three, four, any number of years older."

"That is not a very complimentary speech to make to a young lady, is it?" cries Belinda, but in a faltering ill-assured voice, with the traitor blood still deepening on her cheeks.

"And your dress—all those refined female elegancies with which I have so often wished to see you invested," says Augustus, pompously. "But I suppose, as you expected me to-day, I may, without vanity, attribute a little of that to—"

"Pray don't hesitate."

"—To the very laudable desire of giving me pleasure, my dearest Belinda."

Upon this she lifts her eyes and returns his gaze unflinchingly. "I have taken to refined elegancies, as I have given up paume playing, to suit my own taste. I never thought for one moment of giving you or any one else pleasure—never."

The natural expression, by no means an angelic one, of

Mr. Jones's face replaces in a second all the oily tenderness which, as a suitor, he has thought it wise of late to dissemble. Truth, he feels, is going to be told between him and this keen tongued little vixen at last; and he is quite determined to render truth as unpalatable to her as may be. "Well, Miss O'Shea," looking at his watch as he speaks, "you are not in a particularly complimentary mood this morning, it seems, so the sooner we wish each other good-bye the better. As regards your party in Spain, you will mention to Mrs. O'Shea, perhaps, that circumstances do not allow of my accompanying you."

"I will deliver any message you like to send by me, Mr. Jones."

"I have received a letter that calls me back at once to London, and shall leave this cursed hole with only too much pleasure by the twelve o'clock train. However, I have no doubt you will find Captain Temple a very willing substitute. Before we part, there is one question that I should like, just for curiosity to ask you. *What* was your object in giving me the answer you did, four evenings ago, here, in your own lodgings?"

"The answer!" she stammers. "I don't know what answer you mean. Oh, Mr. Jones, do forgive me if I have offended you!"

"*What* was your object, I ask?" he persists savagely. "Is it so perfectly impossible to you to speak the truth?"

"I answered you more in jest than earnest. You know it. I said that we might try being engaged. We have tried it, and—the thing is impossible. Forgive me, Mr. Jones. I have acted very foolishly, very badly, I know, but I ask you to forgive me. I am wiser now."

"No doubt of it," says Augustus, with one of his odious smiles. "It would be impertinent, I suppose, to inquire under whose influence your wisdom has been gained?"

She stands for several seconds, dumb as though she had

not understood his question; then from throat to temple, the poor little girl turns white, her secret—a secret hitherto to her own inmost conscience—lies bared before her, like a committed sin, in this moment's piercing light. She changes from pale to red, and then to pale again. Her whole childish face works piteously. "I—I am wiser now," is all she can repeat; oh, with what trembling lips, with what scorching irrepressible shame!

"Wiser in one sense of the word, no doubt you are," says Augustus, watching her with contemptuous coolness. "There may be two opinions, perhaps, as to the worldly wisdom of these little changes of fancy. Is it your step-mamma, I wonder, or Captain Temple, who is acting as your adviser? Not your stepmamma, surely."

At the insolence of his tone, his look, Belinda's self-possession returns to her. "My own heart is my adviser, Sir," she cries. "My own heart tells me I could never endure to live a day with you as your wife, let alone a life-time."

"And have you made up your mind—although you do treat me so cruelly I must always take the warmest interest in your welfare—have you made up your mind, Belinda, to live under Captain Temple's roof for the future?"

"I shall do whatever he thinks best for me, Sir." The words stab her; but she utters them with a kind of despairing resolution. "It would be impossible for me to live under the roof of any one I like and honour more than I do Roger Temple."

"Oh! What very delightful sentiments, what charming filial submission! And you were so desperately prejudiced, if you remember. Only four days ago you were ready to quarrel with me for assuming the possibility of Mrs. O'Shea's marriage."

"I did not know Roger Temple then," says Belinda, bravely and simply. "I can excuse Rose now. I think she, or any woman, would be honoured by becoming Roger Temple's wife."

And having got back to the familiar region of truth, the girl's stout spirit rallies. No further blush of shame rises to her cheek, no further tremble of the lip betrays her. Shame was for the first discovery of her weakness. For her love, itself, misplaced, hopeless though it may be, she can feel none. Sure test, oh reader, by which to discover when love is of true metal, and when counterfeit.

Mr. Jones makes his exit; not again to cross the stage of this little drama; and Belinda stands blankly gazing at a world from whence all fair prospectives, all gracious harmonies of colour, seem abruptly blotted out. The cheerful streets—'tis a high Basque festival, and the town is thronged with peasants from the neighbouring villages—the balconies with their gaily-painted awnings, the flush of purple hills across the river, every familiar object upon which she looks seems changed; vivid, intensified, as external objects become in moments of sharp bodily pain, and still distorted to Belinda's untuned jarring sense. Her life is distorted. The gamin life, with its April joys and tears, is over. Over! why, she feels old already; those children playing yonder under the trees, seem separated from her by a score of painful years! The past has died by sudden harshest blow, and she has no future. That is for Rose; for all happy women whose love has been sought for and returned. And then—

—Then across the girl's heart sweep thoughts that are intoxication, memories of words spoken by Roger Temple to "Lagrimas" when there were only the night and solitude to hear, words carrying with them the ring of truth, of earnestness, all unlike the tawdry compliments he lavishes on Rose. Ah, if he care for her ever so slightly, and she may see him sometimes, feel the pressure of his hand, meet the kindness of his eyes, can she not be contented?

Love, in a girl of seventeen, asks so little, expects so little; craves passionately for—it knows not what, yet can live content upon a word, a look, a hand-pressure. Loveliest of human love!—in an honest untutored breast like Belinda's. I say nothing about young ladies reared in a fashionable boarding-school, nurtured on novels, and cherishing mysterious yearnings of the soul towards the dancing-master.

CHAPTER XII.

THE MEMORY OF A KISS.

On reaching the Hotel Isabella, Belinda finds her stepmother alone; dressed in the sprightliest, most juvenile white muslin wrapper, and wearing on the summit of her blonde locks what the Parisian milliners neatly term "a ravishing futility," in the way of cap or badge of widowhood.

"Belinda! and no Mr. Jones? Well, it is positively a reprieve. I am too upset, too miserable, to bear the presence of a man. Oh, my dear girl, think what tortures of suspense I am going through! Colonel Drewe has arrived—is staying in this very hotel."

There is not one of her little poses in which Rose is more successful than that of bashful, girlish perturbation. In her youthful white dress, and holding a microscopic patch of cambric and Valenciennes to her lips, she really at this moment does not look a day over two-and-twenty—in a half-light, of course, and viewed, as every work of genuine art deserves to be viewed, from a proper focus.

"It appears he came by a late train yesterday, but I knew nothing about his arrival till this morning. The poor fellow picked up Spencer's acquaintance in the courtyard, and questioned her; and oh, Belinda! I fear things are worse even than I anticipated! Spencer says the fiery look that came into his eyes when she told him Captain Temple was here, was something fearful."

"Lucky that you can keep out of his way for the day, Rose. There was a beautiful Spanish duchess in this hotel last summer, and six duels were fought about her before the season was over. We must hope Colonel Drewe will have had time to get his fiery feelings under control by the time you come back to-night."

Mrs. O'Shea for a minute or more examines the pattern of her laced handkerchief in silence. "The duty that lies before me is a most cruel one," she sighs at last, looking up with soft remorseful eyes at the ceiling, "I *hope*, in consenting to marry my poor Roger, I have acted conscientiously. I hope it, and I believe it. My rejection of him would have cut Roger Temple adrift from his last moral stay in life. But I cannot forget that there are other, it may be prior claims. . . . You talk of duels jestingly, Belinda! You little know how necessary it is for me to see Colonel Drewe without delay, and alone. For want of women displaying discretion," says Rose, solemnly, "some men's lives have been sacrificed in positions like this."

"But where is he all this time, Rose? Where is this fiery-eyed Colonel Drewe? If you mean to see him before we start you must make haste about it. It is time for you to dress already."

"Ah, my dear child! there is the difficulty. Is it my duty to start at all?" And then, beckoning Belinda to her side, and speaking in whispers, Rose unfolds a series of little Macchiavellian plans by means of which she hopes to mystify everybody throughout the remainder of the day. Roger, in the first place, is to be told that she is suffering from headache, and the party must start for Spain without her. Then Colonel Drewe is to be admitted. Not at first admitted; the wily Spencer must hold him at arm's length with accounts of her mistress' suffering condition until his feelings be sufficiently worked upon. "And then," says Rosie, "I shall take care, you may be sure, to put everything before him in a light as little wounding to his own vanity as possible. My engagement, fortunately, has never been actually given out; and I know, when I have him alone, I can say many things that will soften the blow to him. Poor, poor Stanley! Ah! if I could only persuade him to return quietly to England by this evening's express! Roger need never know more about the visit than I choose to let him know; and —"

"And altogether you will have told one, two, three falsehoods," interrupts Belinda, checking off Rose's "mystifications" on her finger tips. "Three leading falsehoods, and about a dozen small ones. Why have a headache? Why deceive either of them? Why not go on straight, and let everything take its chance?"

"When you are a few years older, child—when you have seen as much of the jealousies of the human heart as I have, you will know that 'going on straight,' as you call it, does not answer. Gentlemen like being deceived, if the deceit saves them from undergoing anything disagreeable; and those women who know how to deceive gracefully—*gracefully*, mind—are always the most popular."

Thus Rose, according to her lights. Looking round amongst your acquaintance in cynical moments, you could almost say that from those supremely unwise lips of hers has fallen, for once, a remark not without its little grain of worldly wisdom.

At the door of the hotel Belinda finds Roger, trying, with rather poor success, to look sympathetic, while Spencer holds forth to him respecting her mistress's headache. Spencer is characteristic; a blonde faded young woman, largely restored by cheap art; as affected as many a really fashionable lady, and with the finest natural ogle in the world. A vile copy— and still a copy, with what a likeness!—of her mistress. Women might look at their lady's maids, as in a mirror, oftener than they think, if they had but common-sense sufficient.

She manœuvres her eyes under their painted lids at Roger; twists her lips out of the form in which God made them; fabricates falsities by the dozen—unnecessary, gross falsities, where Rose had only stipulated for an innocent white lie or two. As the comedy proceeds, an Englishman, tall, of military cut, but with the unmistakable air about him of a man at odds with fortune (Colonel Drewe must surely have fallen in the world of late), peeps through the trellis of vine and jessamine that overshadows the salle-à-manger window close at hand, and listens. He shifts about a little; he turns red; gets one good stare at the handsome, unconscious face of his rival, then draws back, but—alas for military honour that I must confess it—listens still.

"And so Rosie cannot go with us?" says Roger.

"Rosie! He calls her Rosie!" The Unseen takes out his pocket-handkerchief, and wipes his forehead.

"Belinda, what must we do? Put off the excursion till another day?"

"Mrs. O'Shea begs you would on no account do that, Captain Temple," says Spencer. "It is one of her little headaches, you know, Sir."

"Oh! *he* knows, does he?" thinks the gentleman behind the vines and jessamine.

"I'm afraid Mrs. O'Shea and you was out too late last night, Captain Temple. Mrs. O'Shea complained of her 'ead before retiring."

Roger again does his best to look contrite, and again fails signally. "If Rosie really wishes us to go, Belinda? Rosie is so unselfish—never likes other people to be disappointed. Perhaps we had better be guided by her. We shall be a nice little party of three; you, and Miss Burke, and myself—"

"And Mr. Jones," adds Belinda. What on earth should

make Colonel Drewe start so oddly at the sound of the girl's voice? "Don't forget that Mr. Jones has come back from the mountains."

"Jones? Ah! to be sure—Jones," says Roger, in an altered tone. "On second thoughts, I don't know that I have courage enough for the expedition. If Miss Burke were to get me alone among the ruins and begin to argue about the suffrage, I might become a convert to the Woman of the Future before I knew where I was. It will be safer for me to remain behind."

Belinda turns away abruptly. "Amuse yourself well, Captain Temple," she cries, looking back at him across her shoulder. "Mr. Jones is not going to Spain at all; in another hour Mr. Jones will be on his road to England. But, never mind! Burke and I will have an improving day by ourselves. Good-bye! I have not a moment to lose."

Her slip of a figure trips away out of the courtyard, and before she has progressed a dozen steps, Roger Temple has joined her—is on his way to Spain; his terror of Miss Burke, and of her doctrines, it would appear, suddenly overcome. Spencer watches them curiously. Whatever other personage in a love plot remains blind to the truth, be sure that the lady's maid is never long unenlightened. Spencer watches them; drawing inferences of her own as to the future happiness of Captain Temple and her mistress. The stranger, from behind his cover of vines and jessamine, watches them also.

I have said that to-day is a high Basque festival. The country people have assembled, from far and near, in St. Jean de Luz, and it is with difficulty that Belinda and Roger can edge their way along the narrow streets. In an opening beside the principal thoroughfare of the town, one of the great national matches of paume is at its height. The performers are picked men, champions from either side the frontier, and excitement fierce and fiery prevails among the spectators at every thrilling incident in the game. Fifty yards distant a peasant play, or "pastorale," is being acted —the stage, a scaffolding of rough boards, supported on wine casks—before one of the poorer inns. At the turning of the next street comes a procession of priests and singing-boys, bearing the sacrament from church to church. Tambour playing, dancing and inebriety, are everywhere.

Belinda feels in a dream, still: a dream that is no longer one of pain. Her child's life has been spoiled for her, 'tis true; and all the future's gold is for Rose, not her. But she, not Rose, is with Roger now. Their excursion into Spain will last some six or seven hours—six or seven hours to the good, out of a lifetime of separation! Her hand is upon Roger's arm; he insists that she needs his help to get her through the crowd; and his eyes are telling her that she is fair; and her foolish heart beats with pleasure, and she wants nothing on the whole wide earth but what the moment gives her.

Propriety, in the shape of Miss Burke, overtakes them at the railway station. They get their tickets for Hendaye, the last town this side the frontier, and in another quarter of an hour are walking, as well as the scorching breathless heat will allow them, along the banks of the Bidassoa. Here, advised of Murray, their plan is to take boat for Fontarabia —Fontarabia, that looks but a stone's throw distant across the quivering expanse of harbour mud. But man and Murray may propose; fate finishes. They get into one of the unwieldy flat-bottomed boats that ply between France and Spain, are assured by the scarlet-shirted boatmen, in patois only understood of Belinda, that there will be water enough to carry them to Fontarabia this tide, and rather more than half-way across run aground. The boatmen shove, swear, smile. When a Spaniard smiles you may know that your hour is come. "What is to be done? Ah! God knows. This, then, is to be done, as their excellencies insist upon an answer. Either they will remain where they are, some small three-quarters of an hour, and walk ashore on their own legs, or be carried thither in the boatmen's arms now, or they can wait, a matter of several hours, for the return of the tide. Their excellencies will have the condescension to decide." Meanwhile the boatmen take out each a little roll of paper, and prepare, with the most dignified good breeding imaginable, to fold their mid-day cigarritos.

"I vote for being carried ashore at once," cries Belinda. "Propriety, ma'am! What does that matter? I would rather be improper than have sunstroke, any day."

"And I," says Miss Burke, "would sooner perish than be encircled by the arms of those men—of any men. I will never quit this boat, living, save on my own feet."

And not by one hair's-breadth can she be made to swerve from her principles. She will wait till the tide has so far ebbed that she may walk ashore across the mud; will wait, if need be, till nightfall; will risk the danger of sunstroke. To the profanation of a man's, although but a red-shirted boatman's arms, the Woman of the Future will never bring herself to submit.

"Well, if this indeed be the case, then," says Roger, perfidiously; "if we cannot induce you"—induce her!— "to change your mind, Miss Burke, perhaps the best plan would be for Belinda and me to get ashore as we can, look out for an hotel, order dinner, and so on. This will give you more time for seeing Fontarabia afterwards, and—"

"Leave me, I beg, Sir," says Miss Burke, putting up her umbrella, sternly. "But without compliments. Miss O'Shea, I must ask you to dispose of your day entirely without reference to me. Settle with the boatmen? No, I thank you!"—Roger, enslaved by old-world superstitions as to woman's helplessness, having, at this point, weakly taken out his purse. "*I* will settle with them when they have fulfilled their engagement, when I find myself safe on land—not before."

So the matter is settled. One of the men lifts Belinda from the boat, about as easily as a child lifts a kitten, then wades, bearing her in his arms, through the shallow water. Captain Temple is conveyed on the stout shoulders of the other. A couple of minutes later they are ashore on Spanish soil, and alone.

"And now, Señora Lagrimas," says Roger, "what just cause or impediment shall hinder you and me from going to the Alhambra?"

The question is a jest, of course. Unfortunately, just as Roger puts it, Belinda's eyes meet his in one long, wistful, sorrowful look—then droop abashed, and the story is told.

As it s told in ninety-nine cases out of a hundred, reader; the unbidden eloquence of look, or tone, or touch, making itself felt before the lips have ventured on the colder expedient of speech. Well, the intervening space of time that follows, be it of months or minutes, is, I take it, about the most ambrosial of all love's calendar, especially of love that shall never know its earthly end, to which the present is all in all. In well-nigh every other condition of our lives we poor mortals look "before and after:" in this evanescent one of hopeless unspoken passion we are content, fearfully content! No future for us; the whole of the chill years to come spent asunder, and we love each other, we are together now. Perhaps the forlorn rapture of that *now* equals anything that lawfully affianced lovers, with half a century or so of a joint fireside in prospective, ever taste.

They explore the sights of Fontarabia as conscientiously as though they were some prosaic couple whose romance had begun with money considerations and was now yawning itself into extinction throughout a wedding tour. They visit the ramparts, still lying in blackened ruins, as British gunpowder left them. They look down on the classic Three Fords, the scene of that wild night struggle when the Duke won the passage of the Bidassoa, inch by inch, from old Soult. By-and-bye they saunter up to the church through the high street of the town—quaintest little high street, surely, in Christendom, with its flower-decked balconies, and thirteenth century porticoes, and roofs overhanging so far on either hand that scarce a strip of the fervent blue is visible overhead. But they forget two things : to search for an hotel and to order dinner. They also forget the existence of Miss Burke.

The church takes them more than an hour to walk round. Nothing remarkable in the way of art has Fontarabia's parish church to show; the gilded saints and Virgins, the windows, the relics, are precisely like all others of their kind. But these two heretics visit every "station," pause before every altar, slowly, reverently, as though they were admiring the glories of St. Peter's. The mellowed light, the hush, the solitude, seem to shut them away, deliciously to shut them away, from all connection with the glaring, outer world. They linger side by side, silent, not meeting each other's eyes, heaven knows what thoughts filling the hearts of each . . . At length the organ begins to play, a dreamy set of waltzes, followed by an air from one of Verdi's operas. A sleepy-looking priest saunters down the aisle, putting on his gown as he goes; a sleepy-looking chorister boy with incense-burner and book saunters behind. And then in lounges a christening-party, everybody gossiping and laughing with that frank familiarity towards mother church that characterises the whole most Catholic nation. Belinda and Roger make their escape through a side-door, left open by the drowsy-eyed priest, and which leads, down five or six breakneck stairs, into the sacristy.

The sacristy is old, older by centuries than the main body of the church, and is filled with vests, stoles, canopies, dilapidated Beatas, and other ecclesiastical properties of that nature. Our Lady of Pain, in mauve satin, stands at one end ; Our Lady of Delight, in amber silk at the other. The air is redolent of stale incense, mustiness, and garlic—what place in Spain is *not* redolent of garlic ? How if they were to open a window, afford their pagan lungs a little more of heaven's pure air and a little less of the manufactured odour of sanctity ? They open one and discover a balcony, or mural terrace, about twelve feet in length, exquisitely cool, sunless, and siesta-inviting, and with the whole panorama of town, river-mouth, and harbour, outstretched beneath.

"Perhaps, from this height, we shall be able to see Miss Burke about somewhere," cries Belinda, tardily conscience-stricken.

Remark the cruelty of Fate, the pertinacity of that unspiritual god, Circumstance. In the streets, upon the ramparts, guarded at every step they took by an attendant mob of beggar children, they were safe, comparatively ; and in the church, by reason of it being a church, they were safe, comparatively. And then the christening drives them into the sacristy, and garlic and stale incense drive them out upon the balcony, where they are as much alone as they were on that first evening when "Lagrimas" sang her student song under the stairs ; and then, and then . . .

"Belinda," says Roger Temple, somewhat irrelevantly, "don't speak of Miss Burke, child, until the subject is forced upon us. There is something you have omitted to explain to me, and this is a good moment to have it out. Mr. Jones has gone—my profound gratitude go with him. But why? What sent Mr. Jones away?"

"I am sure I don't know—that is, of course I know," answers Belinda, lucidly. "Mr. Jones went—well, because he found there was no good in his remaining any longer."

"I see. You have behaved badly to him, Belinda ;

confess it. Four days ago your dearest hope in life was to possess the Jones diamonds. Don't you remember what you said, that first evening of our acquaintance, the evening when Señora Lagrimas promised to show me the Alhambra?"

She turns away quickly, yet not so quickly but that Roger can mark the conscious reddening of her cheek. "I behaved badly to him, I know, and to myself, too: badly from beginning to end; it makes me ashamed when I think of it. But now—oh! I have grown old and wise, suddenly. It seems a year since you and Rose first came to St Jean de Luz."

"I am sorry I have made your time hang so heavily."

No answer. Though they are talking of Augustus Jones and his diamonds, talking as they might do if Rose or Miss Burke stood by, instinct tells Belinda what supreme moment hurries on apace. And her heart is beating so that she can hear its beats. If her life depended on it she could not lift her eyes to Roger's.

"However, you will be rid of us soon. Spencer is not amusing herself, it seems, and Rose says she does not dare stay more than two days longer. Don't quite forget us when —Belinda, oh! my darling!"

And with this all is over. The tears are raining down her cheeks, and Roger Temple has taken her hands in his, and spoken words such as he never, no, not even in that unlawful whisper beside the hippopotamus, spoke to Rose.

"I have been so miserable," she stammers out her poor little confession presently; "miserable, hopeless, happy, all at once. Don't think badly, don't think altogether badly of me, Sir, and never, never, *never* tell Rose!"

"Think badly of you, Belinda, child! That is the cruellest stab. What, in God's name, do you suppose I think of myself?"

"And you will never tell Rose—I mean when you are far away, and all this is like a dream? You will never tell Rose, and you will not blame me, more than you can help, when you think of me?"

"Blame you, my dearest!" And Roger draws her, shrinking, trembling, with a rapture that is half joy, half fear, to his breast.

The organ plays on and on within the church, and the priest's voice drones out the christening service; and down beneath, on the shore, the fisher children are calling to each other, and far off ebbs and falls the Atlantic. Belinda knows not whether these sounds last a minute or an hour. To human hearts in intense pleasure, as in intense pain, the arbitrary divisions of time exist not. Roger loves her, Roger loves her, and she is with him—her hand clasped in his, his breath upon her cheek, his whispers——

"Montrez-moi les robes de prêtre," cries a voice in rasping tourist French. "Quand j'ai vu, je paie; pas avang."

And into the sacristy, note-book in hand, stalks Miss Burke, her sharp little point of a nose crimsoned by the sun, her boots thick with unsavoury harbour mud. A dirty small boy in a dirtier surplice, one of the functionaries of the church, attends her.

Belinda and Captain Temple come in at once from the balcony. Belinda, to whom, as we know, the small change falsehoods of conventionality are not familiar, hangs her head and is silent. Roger has the extraordinary assurance to express his satisfaction at the meeting, and to add—Miss Burke watching his face, I blush for him as I write it—that they were " looking for her."

"So I perceive," says the lady, curtly. "Looking for me among the idolatries of a popish church! May I inquire whether you have also looked for an hotel and ordered dinner? I believe—I believe, Captain Temple, it was for that purpose that you left me alone in the boat?"

"Well, I—I—the fact is, I don't know that we came across any hotel," says Roger, with an air of penitence. "But if you and Belinda will remain here, I——"

"I have found an hotel and I have ordered dinner," says Miss Burke. "When a gentleman," with withering emphasis on the word, "when a gentleman happens to belong to my party, I invariably take care to see to all practical matters myself. Luckily, I am accustomed to independence."

She turns tartly away, and with the help of her small cicerone proceeds to overhaul the "idolatries" of the place; the vestments, embroidered by loving foolish fingers in many a distant convent cell, our Lady of Delight, our Lady of Pain—all are viewed in the same cold business spirit by the Woman of the Future, and catalogued in the irrepressible note-book for literary use.

Belinda keeps studiously by her side and away from Roger. The sound of Miss Burke's voice, the expression of Miss Burke's eye, have brought the poor child back, roughly, from Elysium to the world of fact. Five minutes ago she was in her lover's arms, happy to the verge of pain, uncalculating of the future, unconscious of either innocence or guilt. He is Captain Temple, Rosie's affianced husband now, and she is divided from him—oh, for ever and ever more! That caress was their first and last. The delight that, beat out thin, is made to extend over thirty or forty years of some women's lives, has lasted for her as long as a kiss lasts, no more. And all the time the organ continues playing; and the sun shines in through the painted sacristy windows; and the children shout still by the river; and the little altar boy, with his picturesque face and dirty surplice, chatters volubly of saints, miracles, and madonnas. The external world as full of sunshine and glad sounds as it was ten minutes ago; and *her* world shipwrecked!

"Alas, how easily things go wrong!
A sigh too much, or a kiss too long,
And there follow a mist, and a weeping rain,
And life is never the same again."

They eat their dinner of strange herbs, garlic predominant, at the one modest posada the town possesses; drink their coffee, or what the innkeeper writes in his bill as coffee, in the street, the whole population, lay and clerical, of Fontarabia looking on; then the quick southern night falls suddenly on plain and mountain, and they must prepare to return. Belinda's promised six hours of happiness are all but spent. All but—how many a fateful turning in our lives is encompassed by those two short words!

Miss Burke insists that she, and she alone, shall make the bargain for the carriage. "Captain Temple undertook to arrange for us about the boat," she remarks. "If we wish to get back to France to-night, the business part of the matter had better now be left to me. It requires moral courage to hold one's own with these shillyshally false-tongued Spaniards, and gentlemen, as a rule, are not possessed of moral courage. I am."

As the sequel proves. After half an hour's hot contest, Miss Burke has succeeded in beating the cochero down to the very lowest fraction for which mortal souls may be conveyed across the frontier to St. Jean de Luz; the fruits of her moral courage being—the oldest, craziest carriage that Fontarabia can produce, with a horse gaunt and shadowy as ever came from Doré's pencil in his illustrations of "Don Quixote."

And here again mark one of those results of hidden causes which we are pleased to call Fate. Had Miss Burke ordered any decent Christian pattern of conveyance, with cattle to match, they had all remained decorously in each other's society throughout the journey; no further whisper, or ghost of a whisper, between Roger and Belinda possible.

But this cranky vehicle is so heavy, the horse so weak, that, long before they reach the frontier bridge at Irun, they are going at a snail's pace ; by the time they commence the ascent of Behobia they have come to a dead lock. The driver descends from his box, swears fearfully in Spanish, French, Basque ; cracks his whip, applies his shoulder, or goes through the pantomime of applying it, to the wheel. In vain. Not a step further can poor Rosinante stir. Their highnesses, these ladies and the gentleman, must make the ascent on foot, if they would reach St. Jean to-night. No help for it. The horse was one of the best horses in Spain in his day, but what will you have ?—to every pig comes Martinmas—his day is past. If their highnesses had only consented to hire a pair !

Roger and Belinda jump out at once; Miss Burke refuses to move, again on principle. The man undertook to drive her from Fontarabia to St. Jean de Luz, and he shall hold to his bargain, if he take the whole night about it.

So Fate has her way. On goes the cranky carriage ; on go the swearing driver and the high-souled Burke ; Belinda and Roger are left alone once more. Alone, but how far more cruelly divided, how infinitely nearer, than when they loitered beside the altars of the dim old church at Fontarabia ! Now has come the moment of temptation in earnest. They have but to turn their faces and the road to the Alhambra lies, straight as road can lie, before them. And in the heart of each is the memory of a kiss !

CHAPTER XIII.

BOHEMIAN HONOUR.

"Take my arm, Belinda; the way is steep."

The way is steep—the loneliness profound. Upon one side stretches forth the Atlantic, silent, at this hour, and motionless, as any little mountain tarn; upon the other are the wild sierras and rocky defiles of the Pass. Behind them, the lights from a score of scattered villages gleaming through the dusk, lies Spain, the land of dreams, the land which even prosaic middle age cannot quit without a sigh.

"And we have not seen the Alhambra after all," says Roger, some minutes later. She took his arm, as he bade her; her hand has become clasped—who knows how?—in his, and she does not seek to draw it away. "Correctness," the outwork of weakness, the prudery born of knowledge, is to Belinda's Arab soul unknown. She is only honest, as yet.

"No, we have not seen the Alhambra"—in rather a shaky voice comes her answer—"and are not likely to see it —together, at all events."

"Six short hours in Spain, and four of those spent with Miss Burke! Now, what can be the use of people like Miss Burke?" speculates Roger, philosophically. "I suppose one ought to accept them without questioning, like heat or electricity, or any other irreducible phenomena. They exist, and that is as much as will ever be known about them."

"I dare say I shall know enough about Burke before I have done with her," remarks Belinda.

"You—you are not going to live with Miss Burke any longer," says Roger, hurriedly, and by no means calculating into what imprudence he will be betrayed next.

"I don't see what I should gain by leaving her, Sir. We are accustomed, at least, to hating each other! I might be worse off among strangers."

"Belinda," stopping short and looking down into her face, "what is the use of talking, or pretending to talk, like this? As if either of us could forget! You to spend the best years of your youth with Miss Burke, and I—great heavens, the thing is a mockery! But it is not too late— my darling, it is not too late. We may draw back yet."

There are few men who make love really well, as regards eloquence of speech; ardent emotion and rounded periods seldom going hand-in-hand, save in the very highest regions of melodrama. But language that in black and white reads trite enough, may easily be alchymised into poetry of a glorious summer night, in a mountain sierra, with the stars shining overhead, and an uncritical heart of seventeen beating time to all you say.

"I don't want to draw back," says Belinda, misunderstanding him. "All this has come upon me—I scarce know how—come upon me, whether I wished it or not. But, if I could, I would not draw back now, for I shall have been happy."

Roger folds her to him in a quick embrace. "And we shall be separated no more, my child," he whispers. "Why, it would be monstrous, for the happiness of our lives—of all of our lives—to be sacrificed for mere want of courage to speak. We shall be separated no more."

He is, I repeat, one of the most chivalrously honourable men breathing. But chivalrously honourable people not unfrequently get themselves in perplexities more stinging than fall to the lot of good, blunt-edged, unrefined common-sense. Many a man, on his road to the altar with an affluent widow of forty, might be tempted into snatching a kiss from some pair of younger, sweeter lips by the way. Roger knows that he has snatched not a kiss only, but a heart, from this poor little girl whom his arms encircle; and revolted conscience hurries him into an atonement more perilous than the crime. To reject Belinda's love—to play the traitor with Rose—either alternative would be intolerable to him in cold blood. But his blood is by no means cold at the present moment; and he can hear the beating of Belinda's heart, and Rose, poor, foolish, elderly, artificial Rose, is an abstraction.

"Never separated?" repeats Belinda, half impatiently. "We shall be separated for ever, Sir, and you know it! Separated, a thousand times more than if you were going to marry a stranger."

"Marry! Don't talk of my marrying. I can never marry any one but——"

The words are spoken under Roger Temple's breath, but they fall, with clearness such as human speech never possessed for her before, on Belinda's ear. She turns deadly white; even with this mask of night upon her face, Roger can see her change of colour. She breaks from his embrace.

"Tell me what you mean, outright, Captain Temple. Say what you have to say plainly. You do not consider yourself bound, then, to marry Rose?"

And thus Roger is forced upon the very horns of the dilemma. Easy to suggest a possible dereliction from duty, by sigh or whisper; horribly hard to put it into language, with the honestest pair of child's eyes in the world looking straight into one's weak, troubled soul. "He had made an egregious error." Something to this effect does he at length contrive to answer her. "During the past dozen years, or more, had mistaken a sentiment for passion, and Rosie, poor Rosie, it may be, had mistaken too. But Rose must be appealed to—the happiness of all their lives left in her hands. She was the most absolutely generous of women——"

"Who—Rose?" interrupts Belinda sharply. "Well, generosity is the last quality I should have assigned to my stepmamma! However, you should know best, Captain Temple, you should know best."

The tone in which the interruption is made, the cruel, mocking laugh accompanying it, are Belinda to the life; Belinda as she used to be before the great transmutor changed all the baser metal of her nature to gold. But Roger's passionate mood is rather quickened than checked by the outburst. What man but must feel secretly flattered by the tender fierceness, the charming rancour, of one pretty woman towards another—especially when he knows himself to be the predisposing cause?

"My dearest little girl," he begins soothingly, and taking her hand again in his.

But Belinda breaks from him impetuously.

"Captain Temple, let us understand each other," she cries, lifting her eyes with piercing earnestness to his face. "After a dozen years' fidelity you love Rose no longer, it seems—are ready to throw her and your fidelity to the winds, and for my sake! Well, now, if this indeed is truth, not flattery, carry it into effect without delay. If we mean to commit a dishonest action let us get it over at once, and without the treachery of soft words—appealing to poor Rosie's generosity, leaving the happiness of all our lives in poor Rosie's hands—bah! *I* at least, am not made of such mawkish stuff!"

"Belinda, child—great heaven! if you knew——"

"Over away there, Sir, not a couple of miles off, is Spain. I know every turn, every short cut through the mountains. What hinders you and me from going to the Alhambra as we planned? Miss Burke will say how she left us, and Rosie, poor Rosie! must guess the rest. Are you ready?"

"Ready?" repeats Roger Temple gravely. Wonderfully has his blood cooled, amazingly has reason reasserted herself under the shock of the girl's audacity. "You are asking me you know not what, Belinda; but the fault is mine, wholly mine. We will, as you say, stoop to no treachery of soft words. I will speak openly to Rose to-night, and——"

"And whatever Rose answers, whatever you may work upon Rose to answer, mind, *I* have done with you!" cries Belinda, in a voice of concentrated passion. "You think you know me because you have amused yourself by flirting with me for half-a-dozen days. Sir—because you have played a few scenes of moonshine love on a balcony, and won me to say what I said to you this afternoon. But you know me no more than the first stranger who meets me in the street. What! You think I would sink so low as to marry you— Rosie's lover?"

"You stooped so low, I thought, as to like me a little," is Roger's reply. "But you are ashamed already—small wonder, God knows!—of your folly."

For a second or two Belinda is dumb. "If I lived fifty years more," she breaks forth then, "if I lived to be an old, old woman, I should never be ashamed of what you call 'my folly.' Never. If—if such a feeling were shameful how could it have come into my heart? I never tried, I never wanted to like you. I knew nothing at all about it till I woke up to-day, and then it was too late to go back, was it not?"

"Too late, indeed," repeats Roger, horribly contrite— contrite as a man might feel who, through blundering accident, had injured a little child for life.

"Well, I can't help what I feel, any more than I can help breathing, but my actions—those are my own. And to think that I would take you by stealth, dishonestly take you from Rose—I, who wouldn't do a sneaking thing to save my life!"

"Belinda, I—"

"I don't pretend to be good or virtuous, you see, for I've been so kicked about, here and there, and have seen so much, and heard so much, that I don't rightly know what virtue is. But whatever game I play, I play it fair. Ask the fellows in St. Jean de Luz if they have ever known me score a false point, or take a dirty advantage of any one. You have promised to marry Rose, and you must marry her, by heaven! Whether you love her or not, you should love your own honour too well to think of change now."

And here, if the reader asks how comes this quality of inalienable uprightness to exist in Belinda O'Shea's heart, a poor neglected little Arab, ignorant of the very A B C of so many ornamental virtues, I answer, I know no more than how the wallflower gets its colour and perfume from the rock. It may be that some qualities of the human soul flourish better exposed to all life's generous chances than under lock and key—that moral growths, like physical ones, have a tendency to elude the barriers of system. The finest wine of Médoc, remember, is raised from a soil where weeds refuse to thrive.

"You read me a sharp lesson," says Roger Temple. "You make me see my own conduct in a fearfully clear light, Belinda."

"Yours? You have not been to blame at all," cries the girl; womanlike in this, that she should sooner guilt rested with her than blame with the man she loves. "You meant only to be kind to me, at first, for Rosie's sake. How could you guess I was going to make such a miserable fool of myself?"

Her voice quivers, breaks down; she covers her face between her hands, and once more Roger's arm, unresisted, holds her close. The embrace lasts for a minute's space or more, and Roger is the first to speak.

"Before we go on our way again, before we go back each to our own path and duty, I want you to say just one word, child—that you forgive me."

"I have nothing to forgive. If I could choose, I would live the time over again since I have known you—yes, up to this very minute."

"And are we going to be friends or enemies in the days to come?"

"I don't know about 'friends.' I shall care for you till the day I die, as I do now."

"And I may have one more kiss—a last one?"

She throws her arms round his neck, without a word.

But Roger does not misunderstand her this time. In the intensity, the abandonment, of that caress he reads aright, that Belinda is taking leave of him for ever.

CHAPTER XIV.

THE CURTAIN FALLS.

And now the closing act remains to be played. Scene, Rosie's drawing-room at the "Isabella;" a lamp or two artistically disposed around the central figure of the tableau; venetian shutters, half closed; a voluptuous fragrance from the magnolias and orange flowers in the courtyard below. Central figure, Rosie, dressed in the palest lavender silk that ever milliner called mourning, with white Spanish veil, with jet comb and earrings, with the bloom of undying youth (warranted) on her cheek. Rosie, light of spirit, satisfied with herself, and with the world, that forms her background, as ever.

To her, just as nine o'clock strikes, enters Belinda, tired-looking, dust-stained, her cheeks paler than her dress, her eyes showing all too plainly the marks of recent tears.

"Why, Belinda, I thought you were never coming back, any of you! And what an object! I am more thankful than ever I did not go. These sight-seeing expeditions are invariably mistakes."

"Utter mistakes," repeats Belinda, sinking into the first chair she comes across. "You have had by far the best of it at home, Rosie."

"It certainly is nice to say one has been in Spain, but

one can say it just as well without going; and as to churches and things, they are all alike ; and you never know what horrid disease you may catch. How do you like me in a veil ? Spencer insists that she has pinned it right; but I am not sure that it should be fastened so high. Now, just see—oh, you must stand up to get the full effect. Do you think *one* inch lower would be more becoming ? Look at me attentively, full-face and profile."

Rosie turns herself slowly round, as the wax ladies with big eye-lashes turn in the barbers' shops, and Belinda watches her with a pang of wearied envy—envy, not of her charms, but of this all-engrossing vanity which so fills and satisfies the creature's whole foolish life.

"Spencer is right, Rose ; it is pinned to perfection. An inch, half an inch, either way might spoil the effect."

"I thought I looked rather well," says Rose, coquettishly surveying herself in an opposite mirror. "But of course in trying a new style one is apt to be nervous. And then I have a horror of anything theatrical. Nothing, I know, would occasion Colonel Drewe such a shock as to find me looking theatrical. He had always the most fastidious taste."

"Colonel Drewe?" repeats Belinda, a little absently. "Ah ! to be sure ; I had forgotten. You and Colonel Drewe have not seen each other yet, then ?"

"No, poor dear fellow. Stanley does not yet know the worst. He wanted to call on me not ten minutes after you had started, but Spencer made so much of my headache— she is really *a fool*, Belinda, when you put her to the test— Spencer made so much of my headache and my sufferings, that at last he took her at her word and went to Biarritz for the afternoon, saying he would call again at nine for certain. Spencer declares the passionate expression of his eyes when he said these words 'for certain,' was enough to make your blood run cold."

"Then I am not wanted, Rose," says Belinda, rising. "If Colonel Drewe is to be here, with passionate eyes, at nine, the sooner I take myself off the better."

But the widow will, for no consideration, be left alone, is coy as a girl of seventeen at the thought of receiving Colonel Drewe—any gentleman—at nine o'clock in the evening unchaperoned. At least, Belinda must stop until the first shock of the meeting, the first agonized shake of the hand, is over; and then—then it suddenly occurs to Mrs. Rose to inquire for her own lawfully affianced lover, whose existence, in the delightful excitement of Colonel Drewe's arrival, she has, to tell the truth, as near as possible, forgotten.

"Captain Temple will be here in a few minutes," says Belinda. Well must she school herself before her tongue can falter out his name! "Miss Burke hired the most horrible old rattle-trap to bring us back from Fontarabia, and Captain Temple and I had to walk a good part of the way. And it was dusty, and—I believe Captain Temple has gone to his lodgings to change his coat."

The girl dissimulates vilely, stammers, changes colour at every word. But Rose's universe at the present moment is comprised in one fondly-imagined vision, Colonel Drewe; and she sees, hears, nothing.

"Dear good old Roger! I can assure you, Belinda, this has been the most harrowing day of my life: first thinking of one of them, then the other. If I had to decide selfishly," says Rose, "if Roger Temple's very life did not hang upon my fidelity, as it does, I am not sure, considering age and standing, and everything else, I should not incline most towards Stanley. Mind, I only say I am not sure. The Temples are a most excellent family; I shall get Lady Olivia Temple to present me at Court next spring; and if there *is* a thing I adore in the world, it is birth."

"Except in the case of Mr. Augustus Jones," suggests Belinda.

"Ah, poor Mr. Jones!" says Rose, in an altered voice. "That was quite a different thing. Money in these days is a kind of aristocracy. I am afraid, Belinda, you have behaved very foolishly about Augustus," she runs on. "I did everything in my power to forward your interests, and now it seems, he has left the place, out of temper with us all. If you throw away excellent chances in this way, what prospect can there be of your settling?"

"What prospect, indeed? Most likely I am fated to be an old maid, Rosie. No use fighting against fate, you know."

"If Roger's disposition were different, I should be willing to offer you a home with us at once. For your poor father's sake, Belinda, in memory of the *tender, perfect* attachment that existed between us, I shall always look upon you with a mother's eyes, and after a time, I shall hope to bring Roger into my wishes. But at present he is so sensitive, morbidly sensitive, I call it, as regards my undivided attention. I am certain he would be jealous, even of your constant presence."

"Very likely. It would be rash, at all events, to try the experiment. And no change of life would make me happier than I am. Miss Burke talks of travelling in Germany, before she begins a fresh book. I may as well travel with her. By the time I have learnt another language or two, I could earn a decent livelihood, could I not, as teacher in a school?"

"Well, there can never be any harm in a young woman acquiring the means of independence," says Rose. "Although, with your means, Belinda, you will at all times have enough to support you nicely. Perhaps," complacently, "teaching *may* be your vocation, my dear. It is not every woman," with a sigh, "who is destined for marriage; and really, those who are not, have much to be thankful for. Marriage, as I know to my cost, is a state—"

But the summing-up of Rose's wedded experiences remains for ever incomplete. Just as she is speaking comes a discreet, lady's maid's tap at the outer door of the apartment, and in another moment, appears Spencer, in a faded grey silk dress, with mock jet cross and earrings, with the downcast ogle of mock modesty; a cheap imitation of her mistress to the last.

"The gentleman who called this morning, ma'am, would be glad to know if you are sufficiently well to receive him?"

Spencer's face telegraphs the intelligence that the visitor, in point of fact, is at her heels; and Rose, sinking a little farther away from the lamplight, adjusts her handkerchief and emotions to perfection point.

"I will make an effort to see this gentleman, Spencer." How Colonel Drewe's heart must thrill at that veiled cooing voice! "I am far, very far, from strong yet; still, if it be a matter of business—"

Another two seconds, and the visitor is midway across the room.

He is tall, just Colonel Drewe's height, and has the unmistakable military air dear to Rosie's heart. So much, without uplifting her eyes, the widow can discern. But what—what ails Belinda! The girl has grown white as ashes; she starts, trembling, to her feet; a cry of doubt, fear, hope, all blent, comes from her lips.

"Belinda, my dear, let me introduce—" begins Rose rising with languid grace from the sofa. "I don't think you and Colonel . . . . Colonel . . . . "

The poor soul turns green under all her pearl powder, under all her fadeless, warranted Bloom of Youth. Well she may! In one of his charming little poems, Owen Meredith tell us how in the lives of most men and women—

"There's a moment when things might yet go even,
    If only the dead could find out when
    To come back, and be forgiven."

But resurrections that are in poetry desirable enough, may prove horribly awkward in everyday prose; especially when comfortable fortunes have been inherited, new engagements entered upon, in the interval. Rose turns green, feels her limbs give way beneath her; shrieks; a good natural shriek, for once, just as she would give at the apparition of a frog or spider. Then, the genius of folly inspiring her, moves a step or two forward, and sinks into the stranger's arms.

"I knew it all along," she gasps out. "My heart told me you were never really, really dead!"

Could the best actress, the cleverest woman breathing, have hit upon a falsity so utter, so conciliatory, so impossible of contradiction? I repeat that folly, transcendent as Rose's folly, scales heights that genius itself can scarce attain.

O'Shea—for it is indeed Cornelius—holds his wife in a sort of rapture to his waistcoat. (It is not a new waistcoat, Rosie sorrowfully perceives. Many cheap cigars have been smoked, much brandy and absinthe consumed, since either waistcoat or coat was new. Cornelius, in very truth, has been muddled in Fortune's moat, and smells somewhat strong of her displeasure.) He bends his head down over hers.

"There are feelings too sacred for utterance," he exclaims. Curious when people feel nothing at all how invariably they insist upon analysing their feelings. "The years, the cruel years of our separation fade away, and it seems but yesterday I held my only darling to my heart."

"But I am changed?" murmurs Rose; the identical remark she murmured on that first night of Roger's return from India. "I am an old, old woman now?"

threadbare coat. She sends up a passionate mute thanksgiving to heaven in her great joy.

"And so Belinda has grown up a beauty, after all," says O'Shea, holding his graceful brown girl at arm's length that he may the better admire her. "But I have seen you already to-day, Belinda. I watched you this morning—little you all suspected it—when you were starting from the hotel. A good-looking young fellow, that, who was with her, Rose, eh? It would be indiscreet, I dare say, to ask his name."

"His name is Temple—Roger Temple," answers Belinda, her face burning with blushes, more for Rosie's sake than her own.

"An old friend of mine and Mr. Shelmadeane's," adds Rose. Poor Rose! She must be really more than mortal could she make this renunciatory speech in a cheerful tone. "I had run down here with my maid to see our dear Belinda, and—and we met Captain Temple—accidentally—"

"As you have now met me, Rosie," says Cornelius, coming with admirable tact, to her rescue. "Quite a chapter of accidents, is it not? But never mind, my love! All's well that ends well, and I shall be only too delighted to make Mr. Roger Temple's acquaintance. This moment," adds O'Shea, looking much as gentlemen look when they get on their legs to return thanks after dinner, "this moment is the happiest—the crown, the finish, so to speak—of my whole chequered life. But let me set myself right in the opinion of those who are dearest to me. I come back, after long absence, after years of reputed death; I find my Rosie, fairer, younger than when I left her, and with her affections still mine, and I am the happiest fellow this side the equator. But," exclaims Cornelius grandly, "had a cruel fate ordained otherwise; had I found my beloved wife in a position where duty demanded such a sacrifice, I would, whatever the cost, have kept the fact of my existence a secret, and in a distant land have prayed to my last hour for the happiness of her from whom Honour, the strongest feeling of which man's breast is capable, held me apart."

Major O'Shea seems to have grown an inch taller during the course of this peroration. He pronounces the word "honour" with the marked emphasis you will frequently observe men of somewhat shifty character attach to it. His daughter gazes at him with fond wet eyes and trembling lips; while his wife—well, I don't want to be hard on Rosie any more, so we will say that his wife too weeps. She holds her laced pocket-handkerchief, at all events, across her face, and keeps up a little running fire of sighs and shudders, and plaintive shakes of the head, which may be interpreted at will.

Just as the family group has arrived at this interesting position, in walks Roger Temple. He is not absolutely ignorant of how matters stand (do you suppose Spencer, with the key-hole sagacity of her tribe, did not know that the visitor was no visitor, but a master, to the full as soon as Rosie knew it herself?) and it must be confessed bears the calamity that has befallen him with a show of manly fortitude that does him credit.

"This—this is Captain Temple." stammers poor Rose. " Cornelius, my dear—"

" Captain Temple, let me introduce myself," says O'Shea airily, and moving towards his wife's friend with outstretched cordial hand : " A dead man may dispense with formalities. Very happy and proud to make Captain Temple's acquaintance."

Who could feel awkwardness long, under the Hibernian sunshine of such a greeting? If we were to conclude that no queer, contradictory pang of jealousy contracts Roger's heart at this moment we should err. I have said already that the existence of a husband, any husband, seems a necessary element of that Quixotic sentiment of his, which he has been so long accustomed to consider hopeless passion;

and the sight of Rose at O'Shea's side has awakened emotions in him such as he certainly never felt during the past heavy weeks when he knew, or believed her to be legitimately his own.

This jealousy, however—jealousy, regret, call it by what name one will—is evanescent as the love itself was unreal. At the first glance Roger meets from Belinda's eyes, Major O'Shea's resurrection seems to him as much a thing of the past as the parting on the Margate beach or the declaration beside the hippopotamus. Five minutes later the restored husband and supplanted lover are chatting together with a friendliness that must dispel Rosie's last lingering dread as to the probability of a duel. In half an hour's time O'Shea is whispering affectionately in his wife's ear—Darby and Joan, together—on the sofa (I have been harsh, too harsh upon Rosie, more than once; it gives me pleasure to part from her in peace, happily restored to a husband's sheltering arms); and Belinda finds herself at an open window, in the further corner of the room, with Roger Temple by her side.

They talk commonplaces for a long time—talk about the clearness of the night, the beauty of the stars, the sweetness of the orange flowers in the courtyard. They keep at a distance, they dare not look into each other's eyes. And all the while they know that they are lovers; that the good-bye spoken between them a couple of hours ago is cancelled; that they are free; and, God willing, mean to pass through the rest of their lives together, hand in hand.

"Time for me to be thinking of the Maison Lohobiague and Miss Burke," says Belinda, at last. "There is Costa, waiting patiently at the gate, as usual, to take me home."

"Home! Don't let me hear you use that word any more in connection with the Maison Lohobiague," exclaims Roger. "You have finished with the Maison Lohobiague and Miss Burke for ever."

"Yes ; I suppose papa will like me to live in England now. Poor papa—if you knew how good it is to be able to say that word again!"

"I hope another word may seem as good to you some day?"

No reply in speech. She only turns to him her dark eyes, shining through a mist of joyful tears, and Roger Temple is contented.

"It cannot be for a long—immensely long time to come." This remark of Belinda's is in answer to a very difficult and momentous question that Roger asks her presently. "In the first place, because of Rose—Rose, who believes your heart to be breaking, Sir, at this moment. In the second, because I shall have to go to school. Do you know, Captain Temple, that I cannot write my own name legibly?"

"I dare say you will be able to sign it, to make a cross, at least, on one important occasion," says Roger, gravely. "I don't get on with learned ladies nor they with me—witness Miss Burke."

"But I am ignorant of everything"

"Except bull-fighting, bolero-dancing, slang in four languages—"

"Ah, don't remind me of all that now!" she interrupts him, with burning cheeks. "If you knew," humbly, "how differently I mean to be for the future! Send me to the strictest boarding-school in Brighton, London, any where you choose—only get a home for Costa, meanwhile—and see if I can't be turned into a respectable member of society, in time."

Roger takes her trembling hand in his and kisses it.

"You shall never go to a boarding-school while you live, child, in London, or elsewhere ; and heaven forbid you should be turned into anything but what you are! There are respectable members of society, and to spare, in the world, already. There are very few Belindas."

So the curtain falls upon this little drama.

Let us hope that the "moonshine love on a balcony" will prove love of the true sort after all : the sort that lasts for life.

THE END.

SIMMONS & BOTTEN, Printers, Shoe Lane, E.C.

S. & Sons.

www.ingramcontent.com/pod-product-compliance
Lightning Source LLC
Chambersburg PA
CBHW032147160426
43197CB00008B/800